Q U I C K   L O A V E S

WILLIAM MORROW

An Imprint of HarperCollins*Publishers*

Jean Anderson

...

Quick Loaves

150 Breads and Cakes,

Meat and Meatless Loaves

HarperCollins books may be purchased for educational,
business, or sales promotional use. For information please
write: Special Markets Department, HarperCollins Publishers
Inc., 10 East 53rd Street, New York, NY 10022.

FIRST EDITION

Designed by Barbara M. Bachman

Printed on acid-free paper

Library of Congress Cataloging-in-Publication Data

Anderson, Jean.
        Quick loaves / Jean Anderson.—1st ed.
            p.   cm.
        Includes index.
        ISBN 0-06-008883-4
        1. Cookery.   2. Baking.   I. Title.

    TX714.A523   2005
    641.8'15—dc22   2004042690

05   06   07   08   09   WBC/RRD   10   9   8   7   6   5   4   3   2   1

CONTENTS

ACKNOWLEDGMENTS

I SHOULD LIKE TO THANK, first and foremost, friend and colleague Joanne Lamb Hayes for assisting with the recipe testing and development. Few food people are more professional, more creative, or more willing to go the extra mile without complaint than Joanne. She is the best.

In addition, I'd like to thank Deborah DiSabatino and my two nieces Linda and Kim Anderson for double-checking a few of the recipes. I'd be remiss if I didn't also acknowledge my taste-testers who played guinea pig whenever there were recipes to sample and appraise: Anne Anderson, David Erisman, Kathy Ketterman, Gina Mahalek, John and Florence Soltys, and the entire Ted and Carrie Waffa family. Thanks go, too, to Sara Moulton, best friend, confidante, and long-time sounding board for her ongoing encouragement and support.

Finally, I'd like to thank Barney Karpfinger, for many years my agent and anchor, who found a home for this book; and my editor, Harriet Bell of William Morrow, for her editorial wisdom, guidance, and enthusiasm. Every author should be so fortunate.

SAY "QUICK LOAVES" and baking powder breads spring to mind. They are loaves, yes. And quick, too. But they are hardly the whole story.

Quick loaves can be sweet or savory, hot or cold, big or little, flat or high-rising, round or square, or shaped like a brick. They can be meaty or meatless, "ethnic" or American, spicy or bland. They can be main dishes, side dishes, desserts. And almost anything in between.

My aim here was to assemble a global collection of quick loaves—the savory as well as the sweet. So what you'll find in these pages are cakes and breads (even a few short-cut yeast breads), meatloaves, vegetable terrines, pudding loaves, gelatin molds, frozen tortes and mousses. Among the recipes are favorites that I've picked up while traveling, old-timers dug out of family files, and entirely

INTRODUCTION

new ones created from scratch. Throughout, I've slashed prep times by streamlining techniques and paring ingredient lists. Some of my loaves do require an hour or so in the oven—but all of them bake unattended so you can go about your business.

To speed things further still, I've created two time-saving mixes: one for breads, one for cakes, neither one freighted with additives. Both can be stored in the freezer or refrigerator and used as needed. Dip into my Quick Break Mix, add a few extras, and presto! County Cork Soda Bread. Or maybe Honey-Glazed Nut Loaf. Or Cheddar-Beer Bread. Or Tomato, Feta, and Olive Bread. Or Whole-Wheat Date–Nut Bread. Only the add-ins change.

Take some of my Quick Cake Mix, stir in a few additional ingredients, and you've got Chocolate–Peanut Butter Crumb Cake. Or if you prefer, Orange–Poppy Seed Cake.

Or Port Wine Cake with Toasted Almonds. Or Apple Upside-Down Gingerbread. Or Peach and Almond Coffeecake. All are created from this one simple mix.

By teaming compatible flavors, I've also developed some herb and spice blends that you can mix in a jif—no more rummaging through the spice shelf every time you make a quick loaf. Why measure out a teaspoon of this . . . and this . . . and this . . . and half a teaspoon of that . . . and that . . . when there's one jar to uncap? One item to measure?

To help break the take-out habit (some of the time, anyway), I've created some easy meatloaves—from a saucy seven-ingredient Muffaletta Loaf to Little Thai Turkey Loaves that bake in just 25 to 30 minutes. There are jiffy meatless main dishes, too—Jalapeño Jack Bread Pudding, for example, and Tofu-Cashew Muffin Loaves with Soy Mayonnaise.

Throughout the book, I share the time-saving tips I've learned in a lifetime of working with food: If you set a gelatin mold in the freezer while you prepare the recipe, the mixture will set up faster; if you shape and bake your meatloaf on a foil-lined baking sheet, there's no messy clean-up. That meatloaf will also bake faster than one in a high-sided pan.

To my mind, nothing has revolutionized the way we cook more than the food processor, especially when it comes to cooking on fast-forward. I simply could not function without one because it reduces to seconds the chopping, mincing, shredding, slicing, and puréeing jobs that have driven us to TV dinners and take-out.

My great hope is that *Quick Loaves* will wean us off of commercial fast food. And that goes for boxed mixes, too.

Cooking and baking from scratch needn't take forever. Or dirty every pot and pan. My quick loaves require very little effort, very little equipment. Yet the rewards are huge.

How to Use This Book

- **First of all, read this entire How to Use chapter. There's information here that you'll need throughout the book.**

- **Before you begin any recipe in this book, read it carefully—twice, if necessary— to make sure that the instructions are absolutely clear.**

- **Before beginning any recipe, check to see that you have all the necessary ingredients and pieces of equipment called for.**

- **To save time, measure the recipe ingredients before you begin cooking. If any partial prep is indicated (peeling, slicing, chunking, etc.), do that beforehand, too.**

- **For baked goods, measure and assemble all the dry ingredients (cake mix, for example, or flour, sugar, leavening, spices, etc.). Because the majority of my breads and cakes call for the muffin method of mixing (combining all the dry ingredients in a bowl, then mixing in the combined liquid ingredients), place all the "wets" (milk, eggs, vanilla, etc.) in a 1- or 2-quart spouted measure so that they can be quickly whisked and folded into the combined dry ingredients.**

- **Do not use one ingredient in place of another unless a recipe specifies substitutions.**

- **Pan sizes and shapes are critical to a recipe's success, so never substitute one pan for another unless a recipe suggests alternatives.**

- **When a recipe says to "cool" something, let it stand until room temperature.**

- When a recipe says to "chill" something, set it in the refrigerator or in an ice bath until uniformly cold.

- Always preheat an oven for 20 minutes, a broiler for 15 minutes.

Unless specified to the contrary

- Eggs are large.

- Butter is old-fashioned, unsalted stick butter. Margarine, "light" or whipped butters, and spreads should never be substituted for stick butter in any of the recipes in this book because they have different shortening powers and may cause the recipes to fail.

- Flour is all-purpose flour—a good balance of soft and hard wheats, not one of the very soft all-purpose, cake, or biscuit flours beloved by Southern cooks. The flour should also be sifted before it is measured and that goes for "pre-sifted" flours, too—all flours compact during shipping and storage. Breads and cakes made with unsifted flour will never be as light and tender as those made with sifted flour.

- Cornmeal is the supermarket staple—granular and yellow.

- Light and dark brown sugars are measured tightly packed in a dry measuring cup.

- Lemon, lime, orange, and grapefruit juices are freshly squeezed.

- Vanilla is always pure vanilla extract, never imitation. The same holds for almond, orange, lemon, and rum extracts. Imitation flavors tend to be perfumey.

- The best freshly grated Parmesan cheese is Parmigiano-Reggiano, but it is expensive. Fortunately, some quite good "Parmesans" are now coming out of Wisconsin and Argentina. They're half the price of Parmigiano-Reggiano and when freshly grated, far superior to commercially grated pseudo-Parmesans.

- Black pepper is freshly ground.

- Salt is uniodized table salt because it's best for baked goods. You can of course substitute kosher salt in the main-dish loaves but increase amounts slightly.

1 *I'VE ALWAYS LOVED* to experiment with food—not only to dream up new food combinations but also to discover more efficient ways of cooking (I grew up, after all, in the Age of Time-and-Motion Studies). Sometimes streamlining a recipe technique did the trick, sometimes trimming an ingredient list, sometimes substituting one pan for another, sometimes jacking up the oven heat, sometimes using a kitchen gadget in unorthodox ways. And sometimes all of the above.

Back when I was a junior food editor at *The Ladies' Home Journal* in New York, I decided—over the protests of colleagues—to slice mushroom caps in an egg-slicer. It worked splendidly and from that day forward we all used the fast egg-slicer method.

BASICS

Another day, confronted with acres of asparagus to peel for a *Journal* luncheon honoring the Duke and Duchess of Windsor, I switched from the paring knife I'd been instructed to use to a swivel-bladed vegetable peeler. It did the job to perfection—and in half the time. Soon after, I discovered that the vegetable peeler was also the best gadget to use for stripping the zest from oranges, lemons, limes, and other citrus fruits.

Like professional chefs who routinely keep a variety of partially prepared foods on hand so that they can send plates into the dining room on time, I stash a number of oft-used items in my freezer or refrigerator: soft bread crumbs for meatloaves and toppings, to name one, and freshly grated Parmigiano-Reggiano, to name another.

My freezer also holds a jumbo-size plastic zipper bag of chopped, skinned, toasted hazelnuts. If you've ever dealt with hazelnuts, you know how pesky they are to skin. To be honest, if I didn't keep a supply of recipe-ready hazelnuts on hand, I'd rarely make my two all-time favorite quick loaves: Toasted Hazelnut Bread (page 68) and Bavarian Hazelnut Torte (page 111). And that would be a shame.

For this book, I've developed three time-saving herb and spice blends that you can make in a minute. Even more important, I have created two quick, multi-purpose mixes that can be stored in the refrigerator or freezer (my own preference), then dipped into whenever you need a jiffy bread or cake. Both dramatically trim prep times for breads and shortbreads, cakes and coffeecakes. Dozens of them.

And there's more good news: my mixes—unlike their commercial counterparts—*aren't* loaded with additives and *are* endlessly versatile.

QUICK BREAD MIX

MAKES ABOUT 5 CUPS

For this mix to serve you well, follow these guidelines:

- Choose an all-round all-purpose flour with a good balance of soft and hard wheats, not one of the soft blends so popular in the South. Those have too little gluten (wheat protein) to work well in this mix.
- Sift the flour before you measure it because precise amounts are critical here—1 cup unsifted flour may actually contain as much as $1\frac{1}{3}$ cups sifted flour.
- Make sure the baking powder you use is fresh.
- If you have a food processor with a large (11- to 14-cup) work bowl, use it for making this mix. You will probably have to cut in the butter in two batches if the mix is to be properly lumpy—about the texture of lentils with a few pea-size lumps among them. If you have no processor, work the butter into the dry ingredients with a pastry blender, again in two batches.
- Use old-fashioned stick butter for this recipe—unsalted or lightly salted, whichever you prefer. Do not substitute soft or whipped butter, margarine, vegetable shortening, or lard. They all have different shortening powers and are not interchangeable with stick butter.

   TIP: *The quickest way to dice a stick of cold butter—and for this recipe it must be ice cold—is to halve it lengthwise, roll it over a quarter-turn, halve lengthwise again, then cut into pats.*

- Measure this mix just as you would flour, that is, spoon it lightly into a cup for dry measures and gently scoop off the top with the edge of a spatula—do not press or pack. There may be a few bumps and depressions because the mix itself is lumpy, but that's okay. Just make sure the amounts measured are as accurate as possible.

▪ Whenever you make a fresh batch of Quick Bread Mix, add any leftovers from the previous batch and mix well with your hands. Then scoop the combined batches back into the plastic zipper bag and set it in the freezer or refrigerator.

▪ When using Quick Bread Mix, do not let it stand on the counter any longer than necessary. It's important to return it to the refrigerator or freezer straightaway. This is especially true in hot, humid weather when moisture may condense in the plastic bag and activate the baking powder. I always try to scoop out what I need directly from the freezer or refrigerator.

4 cups sifted all-purpose flour
1 tablespoon baking powder
1 teaspoon salt
1 cup (2 sticks) ice-cold butter, diced (do not substitute)

1. Churn the flour, baking powder, and salt in a food processor fitted with the metal chopping blade a couple of seconds until well blended. Tap half the mixture onto a large piece of wax paper and reserve.

2. Scatter half the butter evenly over the dry ingredients in the processor and pulse 6 to 8 times. Scrape the work bowl and stir, pushing larger pieces of butter to the bottom. Pulse quickly 3 to 5 times more until the mixture is about the texture of lentils. Empty the mixture into a large mixing bowl.

3. Return the reserved dry mixture to the food processor, scatter the remaining butter evenly on top, and cut in as before. Add to the mixture in the bowl.

4. Toss the two batches together well (along with any leftovers you may have from a previous batch) and spoon into a large zipper freezer bag. Press out all air and seal. Label, date, and store in the refrigerator or freezer. This bread mix will last at least two months in the freezer, a week to ten days in the refrigerator.

5. Scoop out the cold or frozen mix—no need to thaw—and use as individual recipes direct.

NOTE: *If you do much baking, you may want to make two batches of this mix. I often do.*

QUICK CAKE MIX

MAKES ABOUT 7 CUPS

Before preparing this mix, read the headnote for the Quick Bread Mix (page 9). Those guidelines apply here as well.

4 cups sifted all-purpose flour

2 cups sugar

4 teaspoons baking powder

$^1/2$ teaspoon salt

1 cup (2 sticks) ice-cold butter, diced (do not substitute)

1. Churn the flour, sugar, baking powder, and salt in a food processor fitted with the metal chopping blade a couple of seconds until well blended. Tap half the mixture onto a large piece of wax paper and reserve.

2. Scatter half the butter evenly over the dry ingredients in the processor and pulse 6 to 8 times. Scrape the work bowl and stir, pushing larger pieces of butter to the bottom. Pulse quickly 3 to 5 times more until the mixture is about the texture of lentils. Empty the mixture into a large mixing bowl.

3. Return the reserved dry mixture to the food processor, scatter the remaining butter evenly on top, and cut in as before. Add to the mixture in the bowl.

4. Toss the two batches together well, then spoon into a large zipper freezer bag, press out all air, and seal. Label, date, and store in the refrigerator or freezer. This quick cake mix will last at least two months in the freezer, a week to ten days in the refrigerator.

5. Scoop out the cold or frozen mix—no need to thaw—and use as individual recipes direct.

THREE-SPICE MIX

One of my favorite short-cuts is to mix my own spice blends, which can be used in a variety of breads and cakes—sometimes a pinch even does wonders for meatloaf. This one is my "old reliable." If stored on a cool, dark, dry shelf, it stays fresh for several months.

3/4 cup ground cinnamon
1/4 cup ground ginger
1 1/2 tablespoons ground or freshly grated nutmeg

1. Place the three spices in a small bowl and whisk until well blended.
2. Spoon half of the spice mix into an 8-ounce preserving jar, rap against the counter until the mixture compacts a bit. Add the remaining spice mixture and compact as before.
3. Screw the lid down tight, label, and date the jar of spice mix, then store on a cool, dark, dry shelf. Use as recipes direct.

FIVE-SPICE MIX

MAKES ABOUT 1 CUP

I find this mix good for coffeecakes and almost anything containing almonds, almond paste, or marzipan. It reminds me of spice combinations I've enjoyed in Scandinavia, and most of all, in the glorious sweet breads of Sweden. It's not quite as punchy as the Three-Spice Mix.

2/3 cup ground cinnamon

3 tablespoons ground ginger

1 1/2 tablespoons ground or freshly grated nutmeg

1 1/2 teaspoons ground cardamom

1 teaspoon ground cloves

1. Place the five spices in a small bowl and whisk until well blended.
2. Spoon half of the spice mix into an 8-ounce preserving jar, rap against the counter until the mixture compacts a bit. Add the remaining spice mixture and compact as before.
3. Screw the lid down tight, label, and date the jar of spice mix, then store on a cool, dark, dry shelf. Use as recipes direct.

BASIC HERB MIX

MAKES ABOUT 1 CUP

A time-saving, all-round herb blend that can be used in a wide variety of meat, and vegetable loaves, even in some yeast breads and quick breads.

1/2 cup dried leaf basil
1/3 cup dried leaf marjoram
2 tablespoons dried leaf thyme

1. Place the three herbs in a small bowl and whisk until well blended.
2. Spoon half of the herb mix into an 8-ounce preserving jar, rap against the counter until the mixture compacts a bit. Add the remaining herb mixture and compact as before.
3. Screw the lid down tight, label, and date the jar of herb mix, then store on a cool, dark, dry shelf. Use as recipes direct.

TOASTED HAZELNUTS

MAKES ABOUT 2 CUPS

Because I'm so partial to hazelnuts and like to stir them into a variety of quick breads and cakes, I keep a supply of chopped, toasted hazelnuts in the freezer. That way, I don't have to toast, skin, and chop them each time I need them, a saving of about forty-five minutes. Frozen chopped hazelnuts will taste fresh for about two months. The Bavarian Hazelnut Torte (page 111) calls for finely ground toasted hazelnuts. No problem. Simply drop the coarsely chopped nuts into the processor, and using a light touch on the pulse button, pulse until uniformly fine. Easy does it. You don't want to grind the nuts to paste.

1 pound shelled hazelnuts

1. Preheat the oven to 350°F. Spread the hazelnuts one layer deep in an ungreased large shallow roasting pan, and set in the lower third of the oven.
2. Toast uncovered for 10 minutes, stir well, then toast 10 to 15 minutes longer or until the nuts smell irresistible and the bare portions are the color of pale caramel.
3. Remove from the oven and cool 10 minutes in the pan. Dealing with a third or half of the nuts at a time, bundle in a dry dish towel, and rub briskly again and again. This removes most of the skin—don't worry about recalcitrant bits. They'll add flavor and color.
4. Pulse the hazelnuts in two batches in a food processor fitted with the metal chopping blade 4 to 6 times until moderately coarsely chopped. Scrape the work bowl and pulse out any large pieces with a few staccato bursts.
5. Scoop the chopped hazelnuts into a zipper freezer bag and press out all air. Label, date, and store in the freezer. I stash mine on the freezer door where they won't get lost.

Chopped Pecans or Walnuts I occasionally toast pecans (10 to 15 minutes at 350°F) but not walnuts because I don't think toasting improves their flavor. Chop as directed for hazelnuts, using fewer pulses because these nuts are soft. Bag, label, date, and freeze as directed.

GRATE-AHEAD PARMESAN CHEESE

MAKES ABOUT 3 1/2 CUPS

The Parmesan I prefer is Parmigiano-Reggiano imported from Italy, but it's expensive. A surprisingly good domestic Parmesan is now coming out of Wisconsin. So, if I'm feeling a budget crunch, I'll use Wisconsin Parmesan or an acceptable one made in Argentina. I generally grate a pound of Parmesan at a time and store it in a tightly capped 1-quart canning jar in the refrigerator. It's ready to use, it remains "fresh" for four to six weeks, and I think it's better than any of the big commercial brands.

1 pound Parmesan cheese, broken into 1-inch chunks with a cheese wedger

1. Place half the cheese in a food processor fitted with the metal chopping blade and pulse 4 to 5 times—the cheese will be coarsely grated. Snap the motor on and churn until the grated cheese is as fine as you like—10 to 15 seconds for moderately fine, 20 seconds for feathery. Scoop into a 1-quart canning jar, preferably a wide-mouth one.
2. Grate the remaining cheese the same way, add to the jar, and screw the lid down tight.
3. Label, date, and store in the refrigerator.

SOFT WHITE BREAD CRUMBS ON ICE

MAKES ABOUT 6 CUPS

One of the secrets of cooking on fast-forward is to have certain ingredients prepped and ready to go so that all you need do is reach in and scoop up the amount you need. A case in point: soft bread crumbs, which are integral to so many meatloaves. With a food processor, it takes only a few minutes to buzz up a big batch of soft white bread crumbs, which can be stored in the freezer. They'll keep for about three months.

12 slices firm-textured white bread

1. Tear 6 slices of bread into 1- to 1½-inch chunks, letting them fall into a food processor fitted with the metal chopping blade. Pulse 6 to 8 times for crumbs of medium texture—best for most recipes. Empty into a large zipper freezer bag.
2. Crumb the remaining bread the same way and add to the bag. Seal, pressing out all air, label, date, and store in the freezer.

VARIATION

Soft Whole-Wheat Bread Crumbs Prepare as directed for soft white bread crumbs using firm-textured or home-style whole-wheat bread. Bag, label, date, and store in the freezer. Maximum freezer storage time: two months (whole-wheat bread is more perishable than white bread because it contains both husk and germ).

Time-Saving Equipment[*]

To make quick loaves with minimal muss and fuss, I rely on these handy appliances, implements, and accessories:

Food processor Nothing can short-cut the making of breads and cakes, meatloaves, vegetable terrines, even frozen desserts more effectively than a food processor, preferably a sturdy full-size machine with an 11- or 14-cup work bowl. Note that many of my recipes call for a food processor. There's good reason for this. Who wants to chop a couple of onions by hand, a big bell pepper, or a handful of fresh parsley? Not only does the processor perform these tedious jobs in seconds, it can also whiz together the dry ingredients for breads and cakes, then combine the liquids. In fact, it can mix many big, beautiful quick loaves from scratch—almost entirely in the work bowl. If you don't own a food processor, I urge you to take the plunge. You'll be astonished by the machine's versatility and grateful for the time it saves. I also keep a mini food processor at the ready for small jobs—mincing a couple of garlic cloves, for example, a few scallions or sprigs of parsley. It's nice to have but definitely not essential.

Microwave oven The fastest way to thaw frozen food or melt butter; oven wattages vary significantly so let the user's manual be your guide.

Electric citrus juicer Whenever I'm cooking up a storm, I'll juice several lemons and store the juice in a tightly capped glass jar in the refrigerator so all I have to do is dip out the amount I need. Stored this way, lemon juice keeps fresh for about 10 days. I also have a wooden hand reamer and use it if I need a small amount of lemon juice but have none in the refrigerator. The little reamer works equally well for juicing oranges and limes if small quantities are all you need.

Salad spinner This is the most efficient way to wash and dry fresh parsley, cilantro, basil, and other large- or medium-leaved fresh herbs. If I'm going to processor-chop the herbs, I wring them dry in paper toweling after spin-drying because the tiniest bit of moisture will mean "herb paste" instead of crisply chopped herbs.

Large fine-mesh sieve I use a sieve not only for sifting flour but also for washing such tiny-leaved fresh herbs as thyme. The leaves should be patted dry on paper toweling before they're chopped by hand or in the food processor.

Microplane or rasp This piece of equipment—patterned, it's said, after a carpenter's rasp—is just the thing for grating lemon or orange zest, whole nutmeg, fresh ginger, onion, or garlic. The shreds magically fall off the microplane eliminating the need to dig them out of all the little grooves as you must do with an old-fashioned grater.

Swivel-bladed vegetable peeler An old and indispensable friend. Many of my recipes call for removing strips of zest from lemons or oranges, then "grating" them with sugar in a food processor. I hold the fruit directly over the processor work bowl and zip the zest off with a vegetable peeler, letting the strips fall directly into the bowl.

Wire whisk: I use both flat and rounded whisks for combining the dry ingredients of breads and cakes, also for beating the liquids together (milk, egg, vanilla, etc.) until well blended. Of the two, I prefer the flat whisk.

Large and small heat-proof silicone spatulas (or failing these, rubber spatulas) These are essential for folding together the liquid and dry ingredients of breads and cakes, for scraping every last smidge of batter or dough out of a bowl, for spreading batters and doughs in loaf pans, then smoothing their tops. These flexible spatulas (especially small, slim ones) are just the ticket for scraping jam, molasses, honey, salsa, pasta sauce, sour cream, yogurt, and other thick or sticky ingredients out of jars and cartons.

Small thin-blade spatulas Indispensable for leveling off ingredients in dry measuring cups and measuring spoons, also for loosening baked loaves from their pans.

Paring knife, utility knife, and large chef's knife Mainly for prepping ingredients for the food processor.

Serrated knife A good sharp one for slicing meatloaves, breads, and cakes.

Kitchen shears For snipping dried fruits, also spiky or frilly herbs like chives and dill.

Cutting board For prepping ingredients, also for slicing meatloaves, breads, and cakes.

Large mixing bowl For preparing quick bread and cake mixes, stirring up batters and doughs, kneading together meatloaf ingredients, and combining gelatin mixtures.

Nested dry measures 1-cup, ½-cup, ⅓-cup, and ¼-cup sizes. They're not only for measuring flours, sugars, grains, nuts, and other dry ingredients but also sour cream, yogurt, jam, marmalade, and peanut butter.

TIP: *Brown sugar should always be packed into the measure, then leveled off with the edge of a thin-blade spatula. Ditto sour cream, yogurt, peanut butter, jams, jellies, and marmalades.*

The recipes specify exactly which ingredients should be packed into measures.

Measuring spoons For measuring leavenings, herbs and spices, flavorings, and extracts.

1- and 2-cup spouted glass measures For measuring a variety of liquids—milk, honey, molasses, fruit juices, vegetable oils.

TIP: *If you spritz the measuring cup lightly with nonstick cooking spray before pouring in molasses, corn syrup, honey, or other sticky ingredient, you'll find that it will slide out more easily.*

1- and 2-quart spouted glass measures I find these the best choice for combining liquid ingredients for breads and cakes because they are big enough to accommodate them all (milk, eggs, flavorings, etc.) and tall-sided enough that ingredients won't spatter or spew out of the measure as you beat. A flat or small round whisk fits into these large measures comfortably, and finally, the cups' spouts make it easy to pour the blended liquids.

Aluminum foil Oh, so useful—for lining baking sheets and loaf pans, for sliding underneath full loaves that may "boil over" in the oven, for covering loaves that are browning too fast, for enclosing baked sandwich loaves, for wrapping leftovers.

TIP: *To line a loaf pan, turn the pan upside down, smooth the foil over it, shiny side down, mitering the corners crisply, then lift off the foil liner and insert it in the pan. Much easier and faster than trying to line a right-side-up loaf pan.*

Baking parchment For lining baking sheets.

Wax paper To save on dishes, I often measure out dry ingredients on wax paper. I also use wax paper to cover gelatin molds in the refrigerator because it breathes, meaning that moisture drops aren't likely to condense on the paper, then fall back into and soften the gelatin as so often happens with plastic food wrap and foil.

Plastic food wrap The best wrapper for breads and cakes because it keeps them moist and tender.

Plastic zipper bags I prefer the heavier-duty freezer bags because they're less apt to absorb freezer/refrigerator moisture and odors. The jumbo bags are ideal for storing my bread and cake mixes (be sure to label and date each). Plastic zipper bags also keep leftover breads and cakes "fresh" if you press out all the air.

THE PANS AND CONTAINERS I FIND MOST USEFUL

The recipes specify which pans to use and suggest alternatives whenever appropriate.

- **9 x 5 x 3-inch loaf pan: For meatloaves, terrines, breads, and cakes.**

- **8½ x 4½ x 2¾-inch loaf pan: For meatloaves, terrines, breads, and cakes.**

- **13 x 9 x 2-inch loaf pan: For meatloaves and cakes.**

- **9 x 9 x 2-inch metal pan: For breads and cakes.**

- **9 x 9 x 2-inch ovenproof glass baking dish: For gelatin molds containing nuts.**

- **8 x 8 x 2-inch metal pan: For breads and cakes.**

- **Standard muffin pan (with six muffin cups): For mini meatloaves, timbales, individual breads, cakes, and frozen mousses.**

- **Jelly-roll pan: This 15½ x 10½ x 1-inch pan is a good choice for shaped meatloaves because its rim catches and holds the juices that trickle out during baking.**

- **Baking sheet: For baked sandwich loaves, jiffy yeast breads, and a few meatloaves.**

- **9- or 10-inch springform pan: For cakes and frozen tortes.**

- **9-inch round layer cake pan: For cakes.**

- **9-inch round pie pan: For toasting nuts.**

- **Ring molds: For gelatin desserts. The 6-cup mold is the best all-round size.**

- **Decorative gelatin molds: Fluted or embossed with other designs, these dress up gelatin molds. Again, a 6-cup mold is the one I use more than any other.**

About the New Nonstick Silicone Baking Pans

Given the popularity of this revolutionary new bakeware, I retested a number of my quick loaves—breads, cakes, and meatloaves—to determine if these nonstick silicone pans could be substituted for standard metal pans without mishap. Yes—if a few adjustments are made. Here, then, a few guidelines for choosing and using silicone baking pans.

Use only pans made of FDA-approved food-grade silicone. According to the kitchen shop owners I interviewed, there are many brands of silicone bakeware (and more all the time), but the ones their customers like best are Lékué, made in Spain, and Gastroflex, manufactured by Bourgeat in France. For 20 years the European chef's choice, Lékué makes sturdy loaf pans (one somewhat larger than our standard $9 \times 5 \times 3$ and another a shade smaller) as well as muffin pans and deep, fluted Bundt-like molds. Gastroflex specializes in small, fancy molds—for brioches, madeleines, muffins, and such.

Read the manufacturer's instructions before using any silicone pan. And keep these instructions handy for future reference. Most silicone pans must be rubbed with oil or butter before they're used, then again after each trip through the dishwasher.

Because these pans are made abroad, their sizes are slightly off the American standard, thus the recipes in this book may make too much for a pan or occasionally too little. If there's too much batter for a pan, bake the balance as muffins or cupcakes, allowing 20 to 25 minutes. Too much meatloaf mixture? Pat the excess into burgers, freeze, and cook another day. Too little batter for a loaf pan? Bake all of it as muffins or cupcakes.

When filling silicone pans, always leave at least an inch of "rising room" at the top. Do not pack meatloaf mixtures, stiff batters, or doughs into a pan because the sides will bulge and your loaf will be misshapen. Another tip: mound meatloaf mixtures up in the center and make a little trough around the edge of the pan to catch drippings.

Set silicone pans on baking sheets before they go into the oven, and in the case of meatloaves or other mixtures that ooze drippings as they bake, use jelly-roll pans or rimmed baking sheets. Otherwise, the drippings may streak across the baking sheet and down into the oven. It's also a good idea to baste off drippings as they accumulate.

In my experience, the silicone pan in which meatloaves are baked tends to absorb and hold meatloaf flavors. So my advice is to reserve one pan exclusively for meatloaves.

Bake loaves in silicone pans on the middle oven shelf (many of my recipes specify the lower third of the oven, but they were developed using standard metal pans). I find loaves in silicone pans less likely to overbrown on the bottom if baked in the center of the oven.

Because loaves sometimes bake more slowly in silicone than in metal, use my baking times only as a guide. Instead, rely on my tests of doneness and descriptions of how a bread or cake should look and feel when done. In the case of meat and other main-dish loaves, bake to the recommended internal temperatures.

Because loaves baked in silicone pans should cool to room temperature before they are turned out of their pans, you will find cakes and breads exceptionally moist, indeed my more delicate cakes are as soft and wet as steamed puddings.

Silicone pans are easily scratched and cut, so you should never slice a bread, cake, or for that matter, any loaf, until it is out of its pan.

2 *MOST QUICK BREADS*—those leavened with baking powder and/or soda—are mixed by the muffin method. That is, all dry ingredients—flour, sugar, leavening, salt, spices, and so forth—are combined in a large bowl, then a well is made in the middle.

Next all liquids—milk, vegetable oil or melted butter, eggs, vanilla, etc.—are whisked until well blended and poured into that well. Finally, the "wets" and "dries" are stirred together—but only enough to form a lumpy batter with a few floury streaks still clearly visible. These prove that you haven't overbeaten and ensure that your bread will be tender.

Some of my quick breads follow this traditional method. But more of them go to-gether even faster thanks to the make-ahead mixes. These contain butter plus all the dry ingredients—except for spices, nuts, and other add-ins. So you have only to fold in the combined liquids. How hard is that?

QUICK BREADS AND COFFEECAKES *plus* A FEW FAST YEAST BREADS

Another short-cut is to take advantage of the excellent frozen yeast dough now sold at supermarkets. It invites improvisation, so I add almond paste and swirl it into a coffeecake, or sprinkle on Parmesan and herbs and bake it as a bubble loaf or . . . the possibilities are endless. And these yeast breads can be served hours sooner than those made the age-old way.

Finally, I've worked up some baked pizza loaves that begin with a store-bought baguette and end—minutes later—stuffed with meat, cheese, and/or vegetables. They're hearty enough for a light lunch or supper and need only a crisp salad to accompany.

COUNTY CORK SODA BREAD

MAKES A 6-INCH ROUND LOAF

This bread tends to overbrown, so use a silvery baking sheet, not a dark one that will compound the problem by absorbing and holding the intense oven heat.

2 cups Quick Bread Mix (page 9)
2 tablespoons sugar
3/4 teaspoon baking soda
1/4 teaspoon ground or freshly grated nutmeg
1/3 cup dried currants
1/2 cup buttermilk
1 teaspoon sugar (topping)

1. Preheat the oven to 425°F.
2. Using a whisk, combine the bread mix, sugar, soda, and nutmeg in a large mixing bowl. Add the currants, toss well, then make a well in the center of the dry ingredients.
3. Pour the buttermilk into the well and fold in using a large rubber spatula. The dough will be crumbly.
4. Turn onto a lightly floured surface and knead gently, gathering all crumbs and shaping into a ball. Flatten the ball into a 6-inch round and ease onto an ungreased baking sheet.
5. With a sharp knife, make a deep cut along the midline of the dough circle, then a second long, deep cut at a right angle to it. Sprinkle the 1 teaspoon of sugar over the dough and brush all spilled sugar from the baking sheet.
6. Bake in the lower third of the oven until deep brown and hollow-sounding when tapped, 30 to 35 minutes. Cool the bread 5 minutes on a wire rack, cut into wedges, and serve.

BARA BRITH (WELSH SPECKLED BREAD)

MAKES AN 8½ X 4½ X 2¾-INCH LOAF

"Bara" is the Welsh word for bread and none is more popular than this one speckled with dried currants. There are two versions of Bara Brith—a slow yeast-raised loaf and this quick baking-powder bread. As additional short-cuts, start with Quick Bread Mix and take advantage of the ready-to-use, diced candied orange rind now sold in small packets at many supermarkets.

> **2½ cups Quick Bread Mix (page 9)**
>
> **½ cup packed light brown sugar**
>
> **1 teaspoon Three-Spice Mix (page 13)**
>
> **⅔ cup dried currants**
>
> **⅓ cup diced candied orange rind or citron**
>
> **½ cup milk**
>
> **2 tablespoons ginger preserves or orange marmalade**
>
> **2 large eggs**

1. Preheat the oven to 375°F. Coat an 8½ × 4½ × 2¾-inch loaf pan with nonstick oil-and-flour baking spray and set aside.

2. Combine the bread mix, brown sugar, and spice mix in a large bowl, pressing out any sugar lumps. Add the currants and orange rind and toss until nicely dredged. Also separate any pieces of orange rind that may have stuck together. Make a well in the middle of the dry ingredients.

3. Whisk the milk, preserves, and eggs in a 1-quart measure until well blended, pour into the well in the dry ingredients, and fold in using a large rubber spatula. The batter should be lumpy and about the texture of biscuit dough. It's good if there are a few floury streaks.

4. Scoop the batter into the pan, spreading to the corners, and bake the loaf in the lower third of the oven until deeply browned and a cake tester stuck in the middle comes out clean, 45 to 50 minutes.
5. Cool the loaf in the upright pan on a wire rack 15 minutes, loosen around the edge, turn out on the rack, then cool right-side-up to room temperature before slicing.

GRANOLA BREAD WITH DRIED CURRANTS

MAKES AN 8¹/₂ X 4¹/₂ X 2³/₄-INCH LOAF

I use a simple granola cereal made with rolled oats, brown sugar, and molasses—no nuts, no seeds, no coconut.

> 1¹/2 cups Quick Cake Mix (page 12)
> 1 cup Quick Bread Mix (page 9)
> 1 cup granola cereal (see headnote)
> ¹/2 cup dried currants
> ²/3 cup milk
> 2 large eggs
> 1 tablespoon finely grated orange zest
> 1 teaspoon vanilla extract

1. Preheat the oven to 375°F. Coat an 8¹/₂ × 4¹/₂ × 2¹/₂-inch loaf pan with nonstick oil-and-flour baking spray and set aside.
2. Place the cake and bread mixes, the granola, and currants in a large bowl, breaking up any granola or currants that may have stuck together.
   Toss all well, then make a well in the middle of the dry ingredients.
3. Whisk the milk, eggs, orange zest, and vanilla in a 2-quart measure until well blended, pour into the well in the dry ingredients, and fold in—gently but completely—using a rubber spatula. Do not beat—the batter should be lumpy.
4. Scoop the batter into the pan, spreading to the corners, and bake the bread in the lower third of the oven until deeply browned and a cake tester stuck in the middle comes out clean, about 50 minutes.
5. Cool the bread in the upright pan on a wire rack 10 minutes, loosen around the edge, turn out on the rack, then cool right-side-up to room temperature before slicing.

HONEY-GLAZED NUT LOAF

I'm especially fond of this quick bread because it's not very sweet and its texture reminds me of a rustic European bread. The recipe calls for pecans, but English walnuts, black walnuts, or lightly toasted hazelnuts can be substituted.

TIP: *To melt the butter for the glaze and combine it with the honey in a single operation, place the butter and honey in a one-cup ovenproof glass measure, set uncovered in the microwave, and microwave three minutes on LOW.*

2 1/2 cups Quick Bread Mix (page 9)

1/2 cup unsifted whole-wheat flour

1 teaspoon Three-Spice Mix (page 13)

1/4 teaspoon baking soda

1 cup coarsely chopped pecans

2/3 cup buttermilk

2 large eggs

2 tablespoons molasses (not too dark)

2 tablespoons golden honey blended with 1 tablespoon
melted butter (glaze)

2 tablespoons moderately finely chopped pecans (topping)

1. Preheat the oven to 375°F. Coat an 8½ × 4½ × 2¾-inch loaf pan with nonstick oil-and-flour baking spray and set aside.
2. Whisk the bread mix, whole-wheat flour, spice mix, and soda in a large bowl until combined. Add the pecans and toss until nicely dredged. Make a well in the middle of the dry ingredients.

3. Whisk the buttermilk, eggs, and molasses in a 1-quart measure until well blended, pour into the well in the dry ingredients, and fold in using a large rubber spatula to make a stiff dough. It's good if a few floury streaks show.

4. Scoop the dough into the pan, pushing to the corners, then smooth the top. The best tool to use for smoothing is a small offset spatula lightly spritzed with nonstick cooking spray. Bake the bread in the lower third of the oven for 45 minutes.

5. Remove the bread from the oven and pour the glaze evenly on top. Sprinkle on the finely chopped pecans and press lightly to anchor them in the glaze.

6. Return the bread to the oven and bake until deeply browned and a cake tester stuck in the middle comes out clean, 10 to 15 minutes longer.

7. Cool the bread in the upright pan on a wire rack 15 minutes, loosen around the edge, and invert on the rack. Turn right-side-up and cool to room temperature before slicing.

SHORT-CUT CORNBREAD

Crusty on the outside, moist inside, this cornbread reminds me of old-fashioned Virginia batter bread. But it's much, much easier to make.

1¹/2 cups Quick Bread Mix (page 9)

1 cup unsifted stone-ground cornmeal

2 tablespoons sugar

¹/2 teaspoon baking soda

¹/4 teaspoon freshly ground black pepper

1¹/2 cups buttermilk

1 extra-large egg

1. Preheat the oven to 425°F. Coat an 8 × 8 × 2-inch pan with nonstick cooking spray and set aside.
2. Using a whisk, combine the bread mix, cornmeal, sugar, soda, and pepper in a large mixing bowl and make a well in the center.
3. Whisk the buttermilk and egg in a 1-quart measure until well blended, pour into the well in the dry ingredients, then using a large rubber spatula, fold the wet and dry ingredients together. The batter will be very thick—almost like biscuit dough—and if a few lumps and floury specks show, that's fine. Overbeating will toughen the cornbread.
4. Scoop the dough into the pan, spreading to the corners, and bake in the lower third of the oven until golden brown and a cake tester inserted in the middle comes out clean, about 30 minutes. Cut into squares at once and serve.

BUTTERMILK CORNBREAD
WITH BACON AND DRIED TOMATOES

MAKES AN 8 X 8 X 2-INCH LOAF

The dried tomatoes I use for this recipe come in little plastic bags and are labeled julienne dried tomato strips at the supermarket. Because of the rubberyness of dried tomatoes, I find it easier to snip them coarsely with scissors than to chop them with a chef's knife.

> 1¹/2 cups Quick Bread Mix (page 9)
>
> 1 cup unsifted stone-ground cornmeal
>
> 2 tablespoons grated Parmesan (page 18)
>
> 2 tablespoons sugar
>
> ¹/2 teaspoon baking soda
>
> ¹/3 cup crisp bacon bits
>
> ¹/4 cup coarsely chopped dried tomatoes (see headnote)
>
> 1¹/2 cups buttermilk
>
> 1 extra-large egg

1. Preheat the oven to 425°F. Coat an 8 × 8 × 2-inch pan with nonstick cooking spray and set aside.
2. Using a whisk, combine the bread mix, cornmeal, Parmesan, sugar, and soda in a large mixing bowl to combine. Add the bacon and dried tomatoes, toss well, then make a well in the middle of the dry ingredients.

3. Whisk the buttermilk and egg in a 1-quart measure until well blended, pour into the well in the dry ingredients, then using a large rubber spatula, fold the wet and dry ingredients together. The batter will be very thick—almost like biscuit dough—and if a few lumps and floury specks show, that's fine. If you beat them out, you will toughen the cornbread.
4. Scoop the dough into the pan, spreading to the corners, and bake in the lower third of the oven until golden brown and a cake tester inserted in the middle comes out clean, 30 minutes. Cut into squares at once and serve.

JALAPEÑO CORNBREAD WITH MONTEREY JACK

MAKES AN 8 X 8 X 2-INCH LOAF

Use canned diced jalapeños or green chilies with plenty of heat. If the "mild" are all that's available, add half a teaspoon of hot green pepper sauce to the liquid ingredients before folding them into the dry. Also pat the drained chilies very dry on paper toweling before adding to the liquids. This cornbread is so rich it needs no butter.

1 1/2 cups Quick Bread Mix (page 9)

1 cup unsifted stone-ground cornmeal

2 tablespoons sugar

1/2 teaspoon chili powder

1/2 teaspoon baking soda

3/4 cup coarsely shredded Monterey Jack

1 1/2 cups buttermilk

1 extra-large egg

1/4 cup canned diced jalapeños, well drained (see headnote)

1/2 teaspoon hot green pepper sauce (optional)

1. Preheat the oven to 425°F. Coat an 8 × 8 × 2-inch pan with nonstick cooking spray and set aside.
2. Using a whisk, combine the bread mix, cornmeal, sugar, chili powder, and soda in a large mixing bowl. Add the Monterey Jack, toss well, then make a well in the middle of the dry ingredients.

3. Whisk the buttermilk and egg in a 1-quart measure until well blended, stir in the jalapeños, and, if desired, the hot green pepper sauce. Pour into the well in the dry ingredients, and using a large rubber spatula, gently fold the wet and dry ingredients together. The batter will be almost as thick as biscuit dough, lumpy, too, with a few floury streaks. Don't beat these in because if you do, the bread will be tough.

4. Scoop the dough into the pan, spreading to the corners, and bake in the lower third of the oven until golden brown and a cake tester inserted in the middle comes out clean, 30 to 35 minutes. Cut into squares at once and serve.

UPSIDE-DOWN BREAKFAST SAUSAGE LOAF

MAKES 6 TO 8 SERVINGS

It's great to have a repertoire of make-aheads for breakfasts and brunches and this showy cornbread with sausage on top qualifies. It can be reheated by microwave or conventional oven.

1 pound bulk sausage meat

1$^1/_4$ cups unsifted stone-ground cornmeal

1$^1/_2$ cups Quick Bread Mix (page 9)

1 tablespoon sugar

$^1/_2$ teaspoon baking soda

$^1/_2$ teaspoon crumbled leaf oregano

$^1/_4$ teaspoon ground cumin

$^1/_2$ cup coarsely shredded sharp Cheddar

One 10-ounce can diced tomatoes and green chilies (mild, medium, or hot), drained (reserve the liquid) and patted very dry on several thicknesses of paper toweling

Tomato-green chili liquid plus enough buttermilk to total 1$^1/_2$ cups

1 extra-large egg

1. Preheat the oven to 425°F.
2. Crumble the sausage into a 10-inch cast-iron skillet and brown about 5 minutes over moderately high heat, breaking up clumps until the texture of coarse meal. Reduce the heat to its lowest point and keep the sausage warm while you prepare the cornbread.
3. Using a whisk, combine 1 cup of the cornmeal, the bread mix, sugar, soda, oregano, and cumin in a large mixing bowl. Add the cheese, toss well, and make a well in the center of the dry ingredients.

4. Whisk the tomato liquid–buttermilk mixture and egg in a 1-quart measure until well blended, stir in the diced tomatoes and green chilies, and pour into the well in the dry ingredients. With a large rubber spatula, fold (do not beat) the wet and dry ingredients together. The batter will be very thick and lumpy—and a few floury streaks should show.

5. Give the sausage a good stir and pour off any excess drippings. Blend the remaining ¼ cup cornmeal into the sausage, then spoon the cornbread batter over the sausage, smoothing to the edge so that the meat is completely covered.

6. Bake in the lower third of the oven until golden brown and a cake tester inserted in the middle comes out clean, 30 to 35 minutes.

7. Cool the sausage loaf in the skillet 10 minutes, loosen around the edge with a thin-blade metal spatula, and invert on a large round platter. If any bits of sausage stick to the skillet, simply lift them out with a pancake turner and set in place on the loaf. Cut the sausage loaf into wedges and serve hot.

NOTE: *If you don't plan to serve right away, cool the unmolded sausage loaf 30 minutes, cover, and refrigerate. Before reheating, let stand at room temperature 30 minutes.*

To reheat by microwave, place the sausage loaf (or individual pieces) on a microwave-safe plate, cover with plastic wrap or better yet, a domed ovenproof glass lid, and microwave on DEFROST, allowing about 5 minutes for a single large piece and 10 to 12 for the full loaf. If not hot (microwave wattages vary significantly), continue reheating in 3-minute increments. Do not use a higher power level because you will toughen the cornbread.

To reheat in the oven, slide the loaf onto a jelly-roll pan, cover with foil, and set on the middle shelf of a preheated 350°F oven for 15 to 20 minutes.

TOMATO, FETA, AND OLIVE BREAD

MAKES A 9 X 9 X 2-INCH LOAF

Pizza flavors baked into bread. I serve this particular loaf hot—it's perfect for casual meals both indoors and out. The dough is biscuit-stiff but that's exactly as it should be. The point is not to overmix because you risk toughening the tender crumb.

3 cups Quick Bread Mix (page 9)

1/4 cup raw (turbinado) sugar

1 tablespoon Basic Herb Mix (page 15)

1/4 teaspoon baking soda

1/4 teaspoon freshly ground black pepper

1/4 cup dried minced onion

One 8-ounce can tomato sauce

2 large eggs

2 tablespoons ketchup

1/2 cup well-drained olive salad (sliced pimiento-stuffed
     olives)

3/4 cup coarsely crumbled, well-drained feta cheese

1. Preheat the oven to 375°F. Coat a 9 × 9 × 2-inch loaf pan with nonstick oil-and-flour baking spray and set aside.
2. Whisk the bread mix, sugar, herb mix, soda, and pepper in a large bowl to combine. Add the dried minced onion and toss well. Make a well in the middle of the dry ingredients.

3. Whisk the tomato sauce, eggs, and ketchup in a 2-quart measure until well blended, then stir in the olive salad and feta. Pour into the well in the dry ingredients and fold in using a large rubber spatula. At first you'll think there isn't enough liquid—there is, just keep folding lightly until you have a stiff dough with a few floury streaks still visible. Resist the temptation to beat because if you do, you'll toughen the bread.

4. Scoop the dough into the pan, pushing to the corners and smoothing the top. Bake in the lower third of the oven until lightly browned and a cake tester inserted in the middle of the loaf comes out clean, 35 to 40 minutes.

5. Cut into squares and serve hot. This bread is so rich it needs no butter.

PIMIENTO CHEESE BREAD

MAKES A 9 X 9 X 2-INCH LOAF

Like most Southerners, I dote upon pimiento cheese and for that reason, I decided to develop a quick bread using the same key ingredients—coarsely shredded sharp Cheddar and diced pimientos. As with any quick bread, the key to a tender loaf is not overmixing. You want only to combine the liquid and dry ingredients. The best proof that you haven't overmixed is a dough streaked with bits of flour.

TIP: *The easiest way to grate onion is to rub it back and forth across a microplane.*

> **3 cups Quick Bread Mix (page 9)**
> **1 teaspoon Basic Herb Mix (page 15)**
> **1 cup coarsely shredded sharp Cheddar**
> **One 4-ounce jar diced pimientos, drained (reserve liquid)**
> **Pimiento liquid plus enough milk to total 3/4 cup**
> **2 large eggs**
> **2 tablespoons finely grated yellow onion**
> **1 tablespoon Dijon mustard**
> **1 tablespoon ketchup**
> **1/2 teaspoon hot red pepper sauce**

1. Preheat the oven to 375°F. Coat a 9 × 9 × 2-inch pan well with nonstick cooking spray and set aside.
2. Whisk the bread and herb mixes together in a large bowl to combine. Add the cheese and toss well. Make a well in the middle of the dry ingredients.

3. Whisk the pimientos, pimiento liquid–milk mixture, eggs, onion, mustard, ketchup, and hot pepper sauce in a 2-quart measure until well blended. Pour into the well in the dry ingredients and fold in using a large rubber spatula. At first you'll think there isn't enough liquid—there is, just keep folding lightly until you have a stiff dough with a few floury streaks still visible. Do not under any circumstances beat the dough—you'll toughen the bread.

4. Scoop the dough into the pan, pushing to the corners. Bake in the lower third of the oven until lightly browned and a cake tester inserted in the middle of the loaf comes out clean, about 45 minutes.

5. Cool the bread in the upright pan on a wire rack 10 minutes, cut into squares, and serve warm. The good news is that you won't need any butter.

FOUR-WHEAT HEALTH BREAD WITH SHREDDED CARROTS

MAKES A 9 X 5 X 3-INCH LOAF

I take a couple of short-cuts when making this full, dense loaf: I don't bother to sift the all-purpose flour (but I do whisk it lightly before measuring) and I use packaged shredded carrots, which I can pick up at the produce section of my supermarket. If the shreds are overly long (say, a couple of inches), I give them a quick chop with a chef's knife or a brief whiz in the food processor.

1$^{1}/_{2}$ cups unsifted all-purpose flour

1 cup unsifted whole-wheat flour

1 cup raw (turbinado) sugar

$^{1}/_{3}$ cup toasted wheat bran

$^{1}/_{3}$ cup wheat germ

2 teaspoons baking powder

$^{1}/_{2}$ teaspoon baking soda

1 tablespoon Three-Spice Mix (page 13)

1 cup walnuts, black walnuts, or pecans, coarsely chopped

$^{2}/_{3}$ cup canola or other vegetable oil

$^{2}/_{3}$ cup fresh orange juice

2 extra-large eggs

2 teaspoons vanilla extract

2 cups coarsely shredded carrots (see headnote)

1. Preheat the oven to 350°F. Coat a 9 × 5 × 3-inch loaf pan with nonstick cooking spray; set aside.
2. Whisk the two flours, sugar, wheat bran and germ, baking powder, soda, and spice mix in a large bowl to combine. Add the nuts, toss well, then make a well in the middle of the dry ingredients.

3. Whisk the oil, orange juice, eggs, and vanilla in a 2-quart measure until well blended. Mix in the shredded carrots. Pour into the well in the dry ingredients and fold in using a large rubber spatula. Do not beat. The batter will be very thick and lumpy, and there should be flecks of flour showing.
4. Scoop the batter into the pan, spreading to the corners, and bake in the lower third of the oven until richly browned and a cake tester inserted in the middle of the loaf comes out clean, about 1 hour and 10 minutes.
5. Cool the loaf in the upright pan on a wire rack 15 minutes, loosen around the edge, turn out on the rack, then cool right-side-up to room temperature before slicing.

BUTTERMILK BROWN BREAD
WITH OATS AND ROASTED SUNFLOWER SEEDS

MAKES A 9 X 5 X 3-INCH LOAF

Although leavened with baking powder and soda, this faintly sweet rustic loaf has the texture of a slow-rising yeast bread—dense, moist, and chewy. I won't pretend that it's in and out of the oven in minutes, because this particular loaf must bake for a little more than an hour. At least it needs no tending, so you can forget it until the timer bings.

2 1/2 cups Quick Bread Mix (page 9)

1 cup unsifted whole-wheat flour

1/3 cup raw (turbinado) sugar

1 teaspoon Three-Spice Mix (page 13)

1/2 teaspoon baking soda

1 cup quick-cooking rolled oats

1/2 cup dry-roasted sunflower seed kernels

1 1/2 cups buttermilk

2 large eggs

2 tablespoons molasses (not too dark)

1. Preheat the oven to 350°F. Coat a 9 × 5 × 3-inch loaf pan with nonstick cooking spray and set aside.

2. Whisk the bread mix, whole-wheat flour, sugar, spice mix, and soda in a large bowl to combine. Add the rolled oats and sunflower seeds, toss well, then make a well in the middle of the dry ingredients.

3. Whisk the buttermilk, eggs, and molasses in a 2-quart measure until well blended. Pour into the well in the dry ingredients and fold in using a large rubber spatula. Do not beat. The dough will be very thick and lumpy and there should also be a few streaks or flecks of flour showing.

4. Scoop the dough into the pan, pushing to the corners, and bake in the lower third of the oven until richly browned and a cake tester inserted in the middle of the loaf comes out clean, about 1 hour and 15 minutes.
5. Cool the loaf in the upright pan on a wire rack 20 minutes. Loosen around the edge, invert on the rack, then turn right-side-up and cool to room temperature before slicing.

SPICY OAT-AND-APPLE TEA BREAD

It took me four tries to come up with a loaf that's moist and tender from top to bottom. With a scoop of vanilla ice cream—or better yet, dulce de leche—*this tea bread can double as dessert.*

2^1/2 cups Quick Cake Mix (page 12)

1 tablespoon Three-Spice Mix (page 13)

^{1}/2 teaspoon baking soda

^{3}/4 cup pecans, coarsely chopped

^{1}/2 cup rolled oats (quick-cooking or old-fashioned)

1 cup applesauce

^{1}/3 cup milk

1 extra-large egg

2 teaspoons vanilla extract

1. Preheat the oven to 375°F. Coat an 8½ × 4½ × 2¾-inch loaf pan with nonstick cooking spray and set aside.
2. Whisk the cake mix, spice mix, and soda in a large bowl until combined. Add the pecans and rolled oats and toss well. Make a well in the middle of the dry ingredients.
3. Place the applesauce, milk, egg, and vanilla in a 1-quart measure and whisk until well blended. Pour into the well in the dry ingredients and fold in using a large rubber spatula. The batter should be lumpy—no matter if a few floury specks show.
4. Scoop the batter into the pan, spreading to the corners, and bake in the lower third of the oven until richly browned and a cake tester inserted in the middle of the loaf comes out clean, 50 to 55 minutes.
5. Cool the loaf in the upright pan on a wire rack 10 minutes, loosen around the edge, turn out on the rack, then cool right-side-up to room temperature before slicing.

ZUCCHINI BREAD WITH ORANGE AND WALNUTS

MAKES A 9 X 5 X 3-INCH LOAF

When it comes to making quick loaves, the food processor is your best friend, and this recipe proves the point. The machine chops the nuts and zucchini, grates the orange zest, combines the dry ingredients, and blends the liquids. If you had to do it all by hand, this loaf wouldn't be so quick to mix. Once in the oven, the bread bakes slowly, but at least you don't have to babysit it. Just set the timer and go about your business.

1^1/2 cups walnuts

1 cup raw (turbinado) sugar

Zest of 1 medium orange, removed in strips with a vegetable
     peeler

2 cups sifted all-purpose flour

1 tablespoon Three-Spice Mix (page 13)

1^1/2 teaspoons baking powder

^{1}/2 teaspoon baking soda

^{1}/4 teaspoon salt

1 pound small zucchini (about 4), trimmed and cut into
     1-inch chunks

^{1}/2 cup vegetable oil

2 extra-large eggs

1 tablespoon vanilla

1. Preheat the oven to 350°F. Coat a 9 × 5 × 3-inch loaf pan with nonstick cooking spray; set aside.
2. Coarsely chop the walnuts by pulsing briskly in a food processor fitted with the metal chopping blade. Tip into a large mixing bowl.

3. Add the sugar and orange zest to the processor (no need to wash or wipe the bowl or blade) and churn for about a minute. Scrape the work bowl and churn about a minute longer until the orange zest is finely grated. Add the flour, spice mix, baking powder, soda, and salt, and pulse to combine. Add to the nuts, toss well, then make a well in the middle of the dry ingredients.

4. Drop the zucchini into the processor and pulse 6 to 8 times. Scrape the work bowl, then pulse 6 to 8 times more until fairly finely grated. Add the oil, eggs, and vanilla and pulse just enough to combine.

5. Pour into the well in the dry ingredients and fold in using a large rubber spatula. Do not beat. The batter will be very thick and lumpy and there should also be flecks of flour showing.

6. Scoop the batter into the pan, spreading to the corners, and bake in the lower third of the oven until richly browned and a cake tester inserted in the middle of the loaf comes out clean, $1\frac{1}{2}$ to $1\frac{3}{4}$ hours.

7. Cool the loaf in the upright pan on a wire rack 15 minutes, loosen around the edge, turn out on the rack, then cool right-side-up to room temperature before slicing.

BISHOP'S BREAD

It's said that pioneer women, using whatever they had on hand, would rustle up this rich loaf whenever circuit-riding preachers came to call. Small wonder there are so many recipes for Bishop's Bread (some recent versions even include chocolate chips). To save time, I use diced dates, quick-cooking oatmeal, ready-sliced almonds (with the skin still intact), and a package of dried berries and cherries. Only the larger pieces need to be chopped—and coarsely at that.

NOTE: Because this is such a full loaf, I place a piece of aluminum foil underneath the pan lest there be any overflow—so far, so good.

> 2 cups Quick Cake Mix (page 12)
> 1 teaspoon Three-Spice Mix (page 13)
> 1/2 teaspoon baking soda
> 1 cup quick-cooking rolled oats
> One 6-ounce package dried berries and cherries, larger
>   pieces coarsely chopped (see headnote)
> 1/2 cup golden raisins
> 1/2 cup diced dates (I buy them already diced)
> 1/2 cup sliced almonds
> 1 1/4 cups buttermilk
> 1 extra-large egg
> 2 teaspoons vanilla extract

1. Preheat the oven to 375°F. Coat an 8½ × 4½ × 2¾-inch loaf pan with nonstick oil-and-flour baking spray and set aside.
2. Whisk the cake mix, spice mix, and soda in a large bowl until combined. Add the rolled oats, berries and cherries, raisins, dates, and almonds and toss well. Make a well in the middle of the dry ingredients.

3. Whisk the buttermilk, egg, and vanilla in a 1-quart measure until well blended, pour into the well in the dry ingredients, and fold in using a large rubber spatula. The batter should be lumpy. It's good if a few floury specks are visible—they prove you haven't overbeaten.

4. Scoop the batter into the pan, spreading to the corners. Place a 12 × 15-inch sheet of aluminum foil on a rack in the lower third of the oven, set the pan on top, and bake the loaf until deeply browned and a cake tester thrust into the middle comes out clean, 50 to 55 minutes.

5. Cool the loaf in the upright pan on a wire rack 15 minutes, loosen around the edge, turn out on the rack, then cool right-side-up to room temperature before slicing.

CRANBERRY-WALNUT-CHEDDAR BREAD

MAKES A 9 X 5 X 3-INCH LOAF

This is a streamlined version of a recipe given to me years ago by a Vermont farm woman. To make this a year-round bread, I've substituted dried cranberries for the fresh.

2^1/2 cups Quick Cake Mix (page 12)

1 cup walnuts, coarsely chopped

1 cup coarsely shredded sharp Cheddar (preferably a
   Vermont Cheddar)

^{1}/2 cup dried cranberries, coarsely chopped

1 cup milk

2 large eggs

Finely grated zest of ^{1}/2 medium orange

1 teaspoon vanilla extract

1. Preheat the oven to 375°F. Coat a 9 × 5 × 3-inch loaf pan with nonstick oil-and-flour baking spray and set aside.
2. Place the cake mix, walnuts, cheese, and cranberries in a large bowl and toss well. Make a well in the middle of the dry ingredients.
3. Whisk the milk, eggs, orange zest, and vanilla in a 1-quart measure until well blended, pour into the well in the dry ingredients, and fold in using a large rubber spatula. The batter should be lumpy.
4. Scoop the batter into the pan, spreading to the corners, and bake in the lower third of the oven until browned and a cake tester inserted into the middle the loaf comes out clean, 50 to 55 minutes.
5. Cool the loaf in the upright pan on a wire rack 15 minutes, loosen around the edge, turn out on the rack, then cool right-side-up to room temperature before slicing.

PUMPKIN BREAD WITH DRIED CRANBERRIES AND WALNUTS

MAKES AN 8½ X 4½ X 2¾-INCH LOAF

Dried cranberries work better in quick breads than fresh or frozen ones for two very good reasons: they don't ooze liquid and they do keep their rich ruby color.

2½ cups Quick Cake Mix (page 12)
2 teaspoons Three-Spice Mix (page 13)
¼ teaspoon baking soda
½ cup walnuts, coarsely chopped
½ cup dried cranberries
¾ cup firmly packed canned pumpkin (not pumpkin pie mix)
½ cup milk
1 extra-large egg
2 teaspoons vanilla extract

1. Preheat the oven to 375°F. Coat an 8½ × 4½ × 2¾-inch loaf pan with nonstick cooking spray and set aside.
2. Whisk the cake mix, spice mix, and soda in a large bowl until combined. Add the walnuts and cranberries and toss well. Make a well in the middle of the dry ingredients.
3. Place the pumpkin, milk, egg, and vanilla in a 2-quart measure and whisk until well blended. Pour into the well in the dry ingredients and gently fold in using a large rubber spatula. Don't beat. The batter should be lumpy—and it's okay for a few floury streaks to show.
4. Scoop the batter into the pan, spreading to the corners, and bake in the lower third of the oven until richly browned and a cake tester inserted in the middle of the loaf comes out clean, about 45 minutes.
5. Cool the loaf in the upright pan on a wire rack 10 minutes, loosen around the edge, turn out on the rack, then cool right-side-up to room temperature before slicing.

BANANA-BRAN BREAD

MAKES AN 8 1/2 X 4 1/2 X 2 3/4-INCH LOAF

Use ripe, indeed overripe bananas, that can be mashed as thin as cream. I simply purée them in a food processor, then pulse in the egg, vanilla, and lemon zest.

TIP: *The fastest way to grate lemon zest is with a microplane or rasp. I lay the microplane across the top of the food processor work bowl and grate the zest directly onto the other ingredients.*

> 2 cups Quick Bread Mix (page 9)
>
> 1 teaspoon Five-Spice Mix (page 14)
>
> 1/2 teaspoon baking powder
>
> 3/4 cup firmly packed light brown sugar
>
> 1/2 cup coarsely chopped walnuts, black walnuts, or pecans
>
> 1/2 cup bran cereal (not flakes)
>
> 3 very ripe medium bananas (about 1 pound), peeled and cut
>   into 1-inch chunks (I cut the bananas directly into the
>   processor work bowl)
>
> 1 extra-large egg
>
> 1 teaspoon vanilla extract
>
> Finely grated zest of 1/2 medium lemon

1. Preheat the oven to 375°F. Coat an 8½ × 4½ × 2¾-inch loaf pan with nonstick cooking spray and set aside.

2. Whisk the bread mix, spice mix, and baking powder in a large bowl until combined. Add the brown sugar and work in with your fingers until the mixture is uniformly crumbly. Add the nuts and cereal and toss well. Make a well in the middle of the dry ingredients.

3. Place the bananas in a second bowl and mash until creamy. Or better yet, purée in a food processor fitted with the metal chopping blade—an 8- to 10-second churning should do it but scrape the work bowl, then pulse out any remaining lumps.

4. Add the egg, vanilla, and lemon zest and whisk or pulse until smooth. Pour into the well in the dry ingredients and gently fold in using a large rubber spatula. Don't beat. The batter should be lumpy, in fact you want a few floury streaks to show.

5. Scoop the batter into the pan, spreading to the corners, and bake in the lower third of the oven until richly browned and a cake tester inserted in the middle of the loaf comes out clean, 50 to 55 minutes.

6. Cool the loaf in the upright pan on a wire rack 10 minutes, loosen around the edge, turn out on the rack, then cool right-side-up to room temperature before slicing.

WHOLE-WHEAT BANANA–RAISIN BREAD

MAKES AN 8¹/₂ X 4¹/₂ X 2³/₄-INCH LOAF

To pump up the flavor of this bread, I use dried sliced bananas, which my supermarket routinely carries, as well as fresh bananas. I also chop the dried as I purée the fresh using my all-time favorite time-saver—the food processor. Once they're the texture I want, I add the eggs, buttermilk, lemon juice, and vanilla and pulse just enough to combine. A few seconds is all it takes.

> 2 cups Quick Bread Mix (page 9)
> ¹/₂ cup unsifted whole-wheat flour
> ¹/₂ cup raw (turbinado) sugar
> 1 teaspoon Three-Spice Mix (page 13)
> ¹/₂ teaspoon baking soda
> 1 cup seedless raisins
> 2 very ripe medium bananas (10 to 12 ounces), peeled and
>   cut into 1-inch chunks
> 1 cup dried sliced bananas
> 2 large eggs
> ¹/₄ cup buttermilk
> 2 tablespoons fresh lemon juice
> 1 teaspoon vanilla extract

1. Preheat the oven to 375°F. Coat an 8¹/₂ × 4¹/₂ × 2³/₄-inch loaf pan with nonstick oil-and-flour baking spray and set aside.
2. Whisk the bread mix, whole-wheat flour, sugar, spice mix, and baking soda in a large bowl until combined. Add the raisins and toss until nicely dredged. Make a well in the middle of the dry ingredients.

3. Place the fresh and dried bananas in a food processor fitted with the metal chopping blade and churn 8 to 10 seconds. Scrape the work bowl, then pulse out any large lumps.

4. Add the eggs, buttermilk, lemon juice, and vanilla and pulse to combine. Pour into the well in the dry ingredients and gently fold in using a large rubber spatula. Don't beat. The batter should be stiff and lumpy, in fact you want a few floury streaks to show.

5. Scoop the batter into the pan, pushing to the corners, and bake in the lower third of the oven until richly browned and a cake tester inserted in the middle of the loaf comes out clean, 50 to 55 minutes.

6. Cool the loaf in the upright pan on a wire rack 10 minutes, loosen around the edge, turn out on the rack, then cool right-side-up to room temperature before slicing.

APRICOT-ALMOND BREAD SCENTED WITH LEMON THYME

MAKES AN 8 1/2 X 4 1/2 X 2 3/4-INCH LOAF

Now that fresh herbs are available around the calendar in many supermarkets, there is every reason to use fresh lemon thyme in this recipe. If you're unable to find it, substitute one teaspoon finely grated lemon zest. I grate the zest with a microplane, letting the shreds fall into the combined liquid ingredients. The sliced almonds are the packaged ones every grocer sells.

> 2 1/2 cups Quick Cake Mix (page 12)
> 2 teaspoons coarsely chopped fresh lemon thyme or
>   1 teaspoon finely grated lemon zest
> 1 teaspoon Three-Spice Mix (page 13)
> 1/2 cup coarsely chopped dried apricots
> 1/2 cup sliced almonds
> 3/4 cup milk
> 1 extra-large egg
> 1 teaspoon vanilla extract

1. Preheat the oven to 375°F. Coat an 8½ × 4½ × 2¾-inch loaf pan with nonstick oil-and-flour baking spray and set aside.
2. Whisk the cake mix, lemon thyme or lemon zest, and spice mix in a large bowl to combine. Add the apricots and almonds and toss well. Make a well in the middle of the dry ingredients.
3. Whisk the milk, egg, and vanilla in a 1-quart measure until well blended. Pour into the well in the dry ingredients and gently fold in—do not beat—using a large rubber spatula. The batter should be lumpy with a few floury streaks showing.

4. Scoop the batter into the pan, spreading to the corners, and bake in the lower third of the oven until richly browned and a cake tester inserted in the middle of the loaf comes out clean, 45 to 50 minutes.
5. Cool the loaf in the upright pan on a wire rack 10 minutes, loosen around the edge, turn out on the rack, then cool right-side-up to room temperature before slicing.

OATMEAL-CRUSTED DATE AND APRICOT BREAD

MAKES AN 8½ X 4½ X 2¾-INCH LOAF

For this recipe, I prefer to snip the apricots rather than chop them because I like well-defined pieces. For the half-cup called for, you'll need about a dozen dried apricots. The easiest way to snip them is to make a series of vertical cuts in each apricot using sharp kitchen shears, then to make a second series of cuts at right angles to the first. Quicker than it sounds.

2½ cups Quick Cake Mix (page 12)

¼ cup unsifted whole-wheat flour

1 teaspoon Five-Spice Mix (page 14)

1 cup coarsely chopped dates (I buy them already chopped)

½ cup plus 1 tablespoon quick-cooking rolled oats

1/2 cup moderately finely snipped dried apricots (see
   headnote)

¾ cup milk

2 large eggs

1 tablespoon finely grated orange zest

1. Preheat the oven to 375°F. Coat an 8½ × 4½ × 2¾-inch loaf pan with nonstick oil-and-flour baking spray and set aside.

2. Whisk the cake mix, whole-wheat flour, and spice mix in a large bowl until combined. Add the dates, the ½ cup of rolled oats, and the apricots and toss well. Make a well in the middle of the dry ingredients.

3. Whisk the milk, eggs, and orange zest in a 1-quart measure until well blended. Pour into the well in the dry ingredients and using a large rubber spatula fold in gently but completely—do not beat. The batter should be thick and lumpy.

4. Scoop the batter into the pan, spreading to the corners. Smooth the top, then sprinkle on the remaining 1 tablespoon rolled oats. Bake in the lower third of the oven until deep brown and a cake tester inserted in the middle of the loaf comes out clean, about 1 hour.

5. Cool the loaf in the upright pan on a wire rack 15 minutes, loosen around the edge, turn out on the rack, then cool right-side-up to room temperature before slicing.

NOTE: *This bread keeps best if stored in a plastic zipper bag, preferably a heavy-duty freezer bag, with all the air pressed out.*

LEMON-GLAZED LEMON-WALNUT TEA BREAD

MAKES AN 8 1/2 X 4 1/2 X 2 3/4-INCH LOAF

The only tedious part of this recipe is chopping the walnuts but with a food processor the job's done in seconds. For grating the lemon zest, I use that other miracle worker, the microplane.

> 2 1/2 cups Quick Cake Mix (page 12)
> 1 cup moderately finely chopped walnuts
> 1/2 cup milk
> 2 large eggs
> Finely grated zest of 1 large lemon
> 1/4 cup unsifted confectioners' (10X) sugar blended with
>   2 teaspoons fresh lemon juice (glaze)

1. Preheat the oven to 375°F. Coat an 8½ × 4½ × 2¾-inch loaf pan with nonstick oil-and-flour baking spray and set aside.
2. Place the cake mix in a large bowl, add the walnuts, and toss until nicely dredged. Make a well in the middle of the dry ingredients.
3. Whisk the milk, eggs, and lemon zest in a 1-quart measure until well blended. Pour into the well in the dry ingredients and fold in gently but completely using a large rubber spatula. The batter should be lumpy—do not beat.
4. Scoop the batter into the pan, spreading to the corners, and bake in the lower third of the oven until richly browned and a cake tester inserted in the middle of the loaf comes out clean, 50 to 55 minutes.
5. Remove the bread from the oven and immediately brush the glaze on top. Cool in the upright pan on a wire rack 15 minutes, then loosen the bread around the edge, turn out on the rack, and cool right-side-up to room temperature before slicing.

CHEDDAR-BEER BREAD

MAKES AN 8 1/2 X 4 1/2 X 2 3/4-INCH LOAF

What a wonderful quick bread this is. Delicious sliced fresh, delicious toasted. The loaf freezes well, too, and keeps for at least three months.

2 cups Quick Bread Mix (page 9)

1/2 cup unsifted whole-wheat flour

2 tablespoons raw (turbinado) sugar

1 tablespoon caraway seeds

1/4 teaspoon baking soda

1 cup coarsely shredded sharp Cheddar

1 cup flat beer

2 large eggs

1. Preheat the oven to 375°F. Coat an 8½ × 4½ × 2¾-inch loaf pan with nonstick cooking spray and set aside.
2. Whisk the bread mix, whole-wheat flour, sugar, caraway seeds, and soda in a large bowl until combined. Add the shredded cheese and toss well. Make a well in the middle of the dry ingredients.
3. Whisk the beer and eggs in a 1-quart measure until well blended. Pour into the well in the dry ingredients and fold in using a large rubber spatula. The batter should be lumpy—no matter if a few floury specks show.
4. Scoop the batter into the pan, spreading to the corners, and bake in the lower third of the oven until richly browned and a cake tester inserted in the middle of the loaf comes out clean, 50 to 55 minutes.
5. Cool the loaf in the upright pan on a wire rack 10 minutes, loosen around the edge, turn out on the rack, then cool right-side-up to room temperature before slicing.

GREEN ONION BREAD WITH CARAWAY AND CHEDDAR

MAKES AN 8¹/₂ X 4¹/₂ X 2³/₄-INCH LOAF

Choreography is key here: measure all the other ingredients while the scallions and caraway seeds sauté so that you're ready to proceed the minute they're done.

TIP: *If you bunch the scallions after they've been trimmed, you can slice them all at once. A big time-saver.*

1 tablespoon olive oil

6 large scallions, trimmed and thinly sliced

1 tablespoon caraway seeds

2 cups Quick Bread Mix (page 9)

¹/₄ cup raw (turbinado) sugar

¹/₄ teaspoon freshly ground black pepper

1 cup coarsely shredded sharp Cheddar

1 cup milk

2 large eggs

1. Preheat the oven to 375°F. Coat an 8¹/₂ × 4¹/₂ × 2³/₄-inch loaf pan with nonstick cooking spray and set aside.
2. Heat the oil in a small heavy skillet over moderately high heat 1 minute, add the scallions and caraway seeds, toss to coat with oil, reduce heat to low, cover, and cook until scallions are limp—about 5 minutes. Remove from the heat and cool 5 minutes.
3. Meanwhile, whisk the bread mix, sugar, and pepper in a large bowl until combined. Add the shredded cheese and toss well. Make a well in the middle of the dry ingredients.

4. Whisk the milk and eggs in a 1-quart measure until well blended, then stir in the scallion mixture. Pour into the well in the dry ingredients and fold in using a large rubber spatula. The batter should be thick and lumpy—no matter if a few floury specks show.
5. Scoop the batter into the pan, spreading to the corners, and bake in the lower third of the oven until richly browned and a cake tester inserted in the middle of the loaf comes out clean, 45 to 50 minutes.
6. Cool the loaf in the upright pan on a wire rack 15 minutes, loosen around the edge, invert on the rack, then turn right-side-up and cool to room temperature before slicing.

TOASTED HAZELNUT BREAD

MAKES AN 8 1/2 X 4 1/2 X 2 3/4-INCH LOAF

I'm so fond of hazelnuts that I toast them ahead of time, rub off the skins, chop them, and store in a zipper bag in the freezer so they're ready whenever I want them. For directions, see page 16.

2 cups Quick Bread Mix (page 9)
1/2 cup raw (turbinado) sugar
1/2 teaspoon baking soda
1/2 teaspoon freshly grated nutmeg
1/2 teaspoon freshly ground black pepper
1 cup coarsely chopped toasted hazelnuts (see headnote)
3/4 cup buttermilk
2 large eggs

1. Preheat the oven to 375°F. Coat an 8½ × 4½ × 2¾-inch loaf pan with nonstick cooking spray and set aside.
2. Whisk the bread mix, sugar, soda, nutmeg, and pepper in a large bowl until combined. Add the hazelnuts and toss well. Make a well in the middle of the dry ingredients.
3. Whisk the buttermilk and eggs in a 1-quart measure until well blended. Pour into the well in the dry ingredients and fold in using a large rubber spatula. The batter should be lumpy—no matter if a few floury specks show.
4. Scoop the batter into the pan, spreading to the corners, and bake in the lower third of the oven until richly browned and a cake tester inserted in the middle of the loaf comes out clean, 50 to 55 minutes.
5. Cool the loaf in the upright pan on a wire rack 15 minutes, loosen around the edge, turn out on the rack, then cool right-side-up to room temperature before slicing.

WHOLE-WHEAT DATE-NUT BREAD

MAKES AN 8 1/2 X 4 1/2 X 2 3/4-INCH LOAF

Because dates are so sticky and difficult to chop, I buy chopped dates and find that they work well in this recipe. That leaves only the nuts to be coarsely chopped and with a sharp chef's knife, the job's done in a minute or two.

> 2 cups Quick Bread Mix (page 9)
>
> 1 cup unsifted whole-wheat flour
>
> 2 teaspoons Three-Spice Mix (page 13)
>
> 1/2 teaspoon baking soda
>
> 3/4 cup firmly packed dark brown sugar
>
> 1/2 cup coarsely chopped dates (see headnote)
>
> 1/2 cup coarsely chopped pecans or walnuts
>
> 1 1/4 cups buttermilk
>
> 1 extra-large egg
>
> 2 teaspoons vanilla extract

1. Preheat the oven to 375°F. Coat an 8½ × 4½ × 2¾-inch loaf pan with nonstick cooking spray and set aside.

2. Whisk the bread mix, whole-wheat flour, spice mix, and baking soda in a large bowl to combine. Add the brown sugar and work in with your fingers until the mixture is uniformly crumbly. Add the dates and pecans and toss well. Make a well in the middle of the dry ingredients.

3. Whisk the buttermilk, egg, and vanilla in a 1-quart measure until well blended, pour into the well in the dry ingredients, and gently fold in using a large rubber spatula. Don't beat. The batter will be almost as stiff as cookie dough, lumpy, too, with some bits of flour clearly visible. If you overmix at this point you'll have a tough loaf of bread.

4. Scoop the batter into the pan, spreading to the corners, and bake in the lower third of the oven until richly browned and a cake tester inserted in the middle of the loaf comes out clean, 50 to 55 minutes.
5. Cool the loaf in the upright pan on a wire rack 15 minutes, loosen around the edge, turn out on the rack, then cool right-side-up to room temperature before slicing.

SOUR CREAM PUMPKIN COFFEECAKE
WITH PEANUT STREUSEL

MAKES AN 8 X 8 X 2-INCH LOAF

It's more efficient, I think, to make the streusel first and set it aside while you mix the batter. The food processor, alas, doesn't make good streusel—the mixture should be crumbly, and the machine churns everything to paste. My hands did a better job—and in just minutes, too.

TIP: *Use dry-ingredient measures for measuring the pumpkin and sour cream. This way you can pack them into the measure and level off the top just as you do when measuring brown sugar.*

STREUSEL

2 tablespoons unsifted all-purpose flour

2 tablespoons firmly packed light brown sugar

1/4 teaspoon Three-Spice Mix (page 13)

2 tablespoons firmly packed reduced-fat crunchy or creamy peanut butter

2 tablespoons coarsely chopped lightly salted, dry-roasted peanuts

COFFEECAKE

2 1/2 cups Quick Cake Mix (page 12)

2 teaspoons Three-Spice Mix

1/2 teaspoon baking soda

1 cup firmly packed canned pumpkin (not pumpkin pie mix)

1/2 cup firmly packed sour cream

1 extra-large egg

2 teaspoons vanilla extract

1 teaspoon finely grated orange zest

1. Preheat the oven to 375°F. Coat an 8 × 8 × 2-inch loaf pan with nonstick cooking spray and set aside.

2. STREUSEL: With your fingers, work the flour, sugar, spice mix, and peanut butter together until crumbly—about the texture of lentils. Add the peanuts, toss well, and reserve.

3. COFFEECAKE: Whisk the cake mix, spice mix, and baking soda in a large bowl until combined and make a well in the middle.

4. Whisk the pumpkin in a 2-quart measure with the sour cream, egg, vanilla, and orange zest until well blended. Pour into the well in the dry ingredients and fold in using a large rubber spatula—easy does it. You want merely to moisten the dry ingredients. The batter will be very stiff and lumpy. And if a few floury streaks remain, don't worry. These will vanish as the coffeecake bakes. The point is not to overmix because if you do, you'll toughen the coffeecake.

5. Scoop the batter into the pan, spreading to the corners, scatter the streusel evenly on top, and bake in the lower third of the oven until richly browned and a cake tester inserted in the middle of the loaf comes out clean, about 40 minutes.

6. Cool the loaf in the pan on a wire rack to room temperature, then cut into squares and serve.

PEACH AND ALMOND COFFEECAKE

MAKES A 9-INCH ROUND LOAF

My aim here was to create a quick version of the heavenly coffeecakes I've enjoyed in Denmark. This one comes close although Danish cooks would surely use apples, not peaches. You can make part of the topping—the streusel-like mix of almond paste, flour, sugar, and spice mix—well ahead of time and refrigerate until ready to use. You can combine these four ingredients in a food processor using long pulses—15 to 20 in all to get just the right crumbly texture. I thaw the peaches overnight in the fridge, placing them in a large fine sieve set over a bowl. The little bit of drained-off peach liquid goes into the batter. The food processor (or an electric blender) is the fastest way to combine the batter's liquid ingredients because they buzz the almond paste to smoothness. A hand electric mixer is slower going and you won't get as smooth a blend.

TOPPING

1/2 of a 7-ounce roll almond paste, crumbled

1/4 cup unsifted all-purpose flour

1/4 cup sugar

1/2 teaspoon Five-Spice Mix (page 14)

One 16-ounce package frozen unsweetened sliced peaches,
     thawed, drained, liquid reserved, and peaches patted
     very dry on paper toweling

3 tablespoons sliced almonds

COFFEECAKE

2^1/2 cups Quick Cake Mix (page 12)

^{1}/4 of a 7-ounce roll almond paste, crumbled

Liquid from the thawed peaches plus enough milk to total

   ^{2}/3 cup

1 teaspoon vanilla extract

^{1}/4 teaspoon almond extract

1 extra-large egg

1. Preheat the oven to 375°F. Coat a 9-inch springform pan with nonstick cooking spray; set aside.
2. TOPPING: With your fingers, work the almond paste, flour, sugar, and spice mix together until the texture of lentils (or pulse in a food processor). Set aside.
3. COFFEECAKE: Place the cake mix in a large bowl and make a well in the center. Churn the almond paste, peach liquid–milk mixture, and vanilla and almond extracts in a food processor or electric blender a few seconds until well blended. Scrape the work bowl or blender cup, then pulse out any lumps. Add the egg and incorporate with a few quick pulses.
4. Pour into the well in the dry ingredients and fold in using a large rubber spatula—you want merely to moisten the dry ingredients. The batter will be very stiff and lumpy with a few floury streaks visible. Do not beat—if you overmix, the coffeecake will be tough.
5. Scoop the batter into the pan, spreading to the edge. Scatter half the reserved almond paste topping mixture evenly over the batter, then spiral the sliced peaches on top. Scatter with the remaining almond paste topping mixture and strew with the sliced almonds.

6. Set on a baking sheet and bake in the lower third of the oven until lightly browned and a cake tester inserted in the center of the coffeecake comes out clean, 50 to 55 minutes.
7. Cool the coffeecake in the pan on a wire rack 30 minutes. Loosen around the edge with a thin-blade metal spatula, release, and remove the springform pan sides. Cut the coffeecake into wedges and serve.

ALMOND SWIRL COFFEECAKE

MAKES 6 TO 8 SERVINGS

I find frozen bread dough—a supermarket staple across much of the country—a delicious time-saver (just thaw it overnight in the refrigerator). Moreover, it's endlessly versatile. This showy coffeecake goes together zip-quick, rises in a shade over half an hour, and bakes even faster.

COFFEECAKE

One 1-pound loaf frozen white bread dough, thawed and at
room temperature
One 7-ounce package almond paste
4 to 5 tablespoons half-and-half
1/2 teaspoon Five-Spice Mix (page 14)
1/2 cup sliced almonds

GLAZE

1/2 cup unsifted confectioners' (10X) sugar
1 1/2 to 2 teaspoons water
1/4 teaspoon almond extract

1. COFFEECAKE: Roll the dough on a lightly floured surface into a 15 × 10-inch rectangle. The dough will be elastic and keep pulling back, but persist and if necessary, let the dough rest 5 minutes to relax the gluten.
2. Crumble the almond paste into a small bowl and gradually blend in enough half-and-half for good spreading consistency. Spread over the dough leaving no margins. Sprinkle with the spice mix and all but 1 tablespoon of the sliced almonds. Roll the dough up jelly-roll style, forming a log 10 inches long.
3. Coat a baking sheet with nonstick cooking spray and ease the log onto it. With a sharp knife, make 11 slashes across the log, spacing them evenly, cutting to

within ½ inch of the bottom, and forming slices that can be twisted to reveal a pinwheel design. Pull the slices of dough alternately to the left and right. Cover loosely with wax paper and let rise in a warm spot away from drafts until the coffeecake begins to puff, 30 to 35 minutes.

4. Toward the end of the rising period, preheat the oven to 400°F. Bake the coffeecake on the middle oven shelf until richly browned and hollow-sounding when thumped, 20 to 25 minutes.

5. Ease the coffeecake from the pan onto a wire rack set over a wax paper–covered counter and cool 10 minutes.

6. While the cake is cooling, whisk all glaze ingredients together.

7. Drizzle the glaze decoratively over the coffeecake and sprinkle with the 1 tablespoon reserved sliced almonds. Let the glaze dry 10 minutes, then slice the coffeecake and serve warm.

ORANGE-WALNUT SUNDAY BREAKFAST BREAD

MAKES A 14 X 4 X 2-INCH LOAF

Here's another jiffy yeast bread that begins with frozen supermarket dough. This time I use whole-wheat, but white bread dough works just as well. The quickest way to grate the zest is with a microplane.

TIP: If you thaw frozen bread dough in the fridge overnight, it will be ready for you in the morning.

One 1-pound loaf frozen whole-wheat bread dough, thawed
$1/2$ cup packed light brown sugar
$1/4$ cup ($1/2$ stick) butter, at room temperature
1 tablespoon finely grated orange zest
1 teaspoon Three-Spice Mix (page 13)
$1/2$ cup finely chopped walnuts

1. Preheat the oven to 375°F. Line a baking sheet with aluminum foil, dull side up, and spritz the foil lightly with nonstick cooking spray.
2. Center the loaf of dough on the pan, then with a sharp knife, slash crosswise and on the bias at 1-inch intervals, cutting to but not through the bottom. Spread the slices.
3. Cream the sugar, butter, orange zest, and spice mix in a small bowl until smooth, then mix in the walnuts, and spread lavishly on each slice. Reserve any unused walnut mixture. Cover loosely with wax paper and set in a warm, draft-free spot until the loaf begins to rise, about 30 minutes.
4. Bake the bread on the middle oven shelf until richly browned and hollow-sounding when thumped, 25 to 30 minutes.
5. Cool 5 to 10 minutes on the baking sheet, then serve warm. Scoop any remaining walnut mixture into a small bowl and pass separately so that everyone can help himself to more.

HERBED PARMESAN AND GARLIC BREAD

MAKES A 14 X 4 X 2-INCH LOAF

Frozen whole-wheat and white bread dough are both delicious prepared this zip-quick way. It's your call. If you want an even gutsier garlic bread, use two large cloves instead of one. You might also substitute grated pecorino Romano for Parmesan.

One 1-pound loaf frozen whole-wheat or white bread dough,
    thawed
1/4 cup grated Parmesan (page 18)
3 tablespoons butter, at room temperature
1 large garlic clove, crushed (see headnote)
1 teaspoon Basic Herb Mix (page 15)
1/4 teaspoon freshly ground black pepper

1. Preheat the oven to 375°F. Line a baking sheet with aluminum foil, dull side up, and lightly coat the foil with nonstick cooking spray.
2. Center the loaf of dough on the pan, then with a sharp knife, slash crosswise and on the bias at 1-inch intervals, cutting to but not through the bottom. Spread the slices.
3. Combine all remaining ingredients in a small bowl and spread generously on each slice. Cover loosely with wax paper and set in a warm, draft-free spot until the loaf begins to rise, about 30 minutes,
4. Bake the bread on the middle oven shelf until richly browned and hollow-sounding when thumped, 25 to 30 minutes.
5. Cool 5 to 10 minutes on the baking sheet. Halve the loaf crosswise, nestle the two halves in a napkin-lined basket, and serve.

MUSHROOM PARTY BAGUETTES

MAKES TWO 13- TO 15-INCH BAGUETTES

I often serve these loaves in place of garlic bread. A big plus is that you can ready the loaves a couple of hours ahead of time, wrap them in foil, and refrigerate until you're ready to proceed, but note that the cold loaves will probably need an extra ten minutes in the oven. The fastest way to chop the scallions, garlic, and mushrooms is in a food processor. I cut the scallions in one-inch chunks and pulse with the garlic until fairly fine, then add the mushrooms and chop these fine, too—eight to ten pulses is all it takes, but I do scrape the work bowl well at halftime.

> **Two 9- to 12-ounce baguettes (13 to 15 inches long)**
> **3 tablespoons olive oil**
> **One 8-ounce package sliced white mushrooms,**
>   **finely chopped (see headnote)**
> **6 medium scallions, trimmed and finely chopped**
>   **(include some green tops)**
> **1 small garlic clove, finely chopped**
> **1/2 teaspoon salt**
> **1/4 teaspoon finely ground black pepper**

1. Preheat the oven to 400°F. Slice each baguette crosswise and on the bias at 1-inch intervals, cutting to but not through the bottom crust. Center each loaf on a sheet of heavy-duty aluminum foil large enough to enclose it and set aside.

2. Heat the olive oil in a heavy medium skillet over high heat 1 minute, add the mushrooms, scallions, garlic, salt, and pepper, and stir-fry 1 minute. Reduce the heat to low, cover, and cook 10 minutes. Uncover and cook until all liquid evaporates, 1 to 2 minutes.

3. "Butter" each baguette slice with the mushroom mixture, wrap the loaves snugly in foil, and bake in the lower third of the oven for 30 minutes. Unwrap and serve hot.

LITTLE PIZZA LOAVES

MAKES 4 SERVINGS

Use any favorite tomato-based pasta sauce for this recipe—bottled or homemade. And be sure to try the quick and easy variations.

TIP: *To save clean-up, line the baking sheet with foil.*

> **One 9- to 12-ounce baguette (13 to 15 inches long)**
> **2 tablespoons olive oil**
> **1 cup pasta sauce**
> **2 teaspoons Basic Herb Mix (page 15)**
> **3/4 cup coarsely shredded mozzarella**

1. Preheat the oven to 400°F. Line a baking sheet with aluminum foil, placing dull side up.
2. Halve the baguette crosswise, then halve each half lengthwise. Place the four pieces of baguette on the baking sheet, cut side up, and brush each with the olive oil. Bake on the middle oven shelf 6 to 8 minutes, until lightly toasted.
3. Remove from the oven, spread each piece of baguette with ¼ cup of the pasta sauce, then sprinkle each with ½ teaspoon of the herb mix and 3 tablespoons of the mozzarella.
4. Return to the oven and bake just until the cheese melts, 10 to 12 minutes. Serve at once.

VARIATIONS

Little Mushroom Pizza Loaves Thaw one 12-ounce package frozen sliced mushrooms, drain, then press out as much liquid as possible. Heat 1 tablespoon olive oil in a heavy medium skillet over high heat 1 minute, add the mushrooms and 1 teaspoon Basic Herb Mix and stir-fry 1 minute. Reduce the heat to low and cook the mushrooms, stirring occasionally, until almost all liquid evaporates, 3 to 5 minutes; set aside. Prepare the basic recipe as directed through Step 2. Remove from the oven, spread each piece of baguette with ¼ cup of the pasta sauce, and sprinkle with 2 tablespoons coarsely shredded mozzarella. Arrange the mushrooms on top, dividing equally, then sprinkle each with 1 more tablespoon mozzarella. Bake as directed in Step 4 and serve.

Little Pepperoni Pizza Loaves Cook 24 thin slices of pepperoni in a large heavy skillet over moderate heat 3 to 4 minutes until most of the fat oozes out; drain on paper toweling. Prepare the basic recipe as directed through Step 2. Remove from the oven, spread each piece of baguette with ¼ cup of the pasta sauce and sprinkle with 2 tablespoons coarsely shredded mozzarella. Top each little loaf with 6 slices of pepperoni, overlapping slightly, then sprinkle each with 1 more tablespoon mozzarella. Bake as directed in Step 4 and serve.

Little Pepper and Onion Pizza Loaves Thaw one half of a 1-pound package frozen bell pepper—onion stir-fry mix, drain, then press out as much liquid as possible. Heat 1 tablespoon olive oil in a heavy medium skillet over high heat 1 minute, add the stir-fry mix and 1 teaspoon Basic Herb Mix and stir-fry 1 minute. Reduce the heat to low and cook, stirring occasionally, until nearly all liquid evaporates, 3 to 5 minutes. Set aside. Prepare the basic recipe as directed through Step 2. Remove from the oven, spread each piece of baguette with ¼ cup of the pasta sauce and sprinkle with 2 tablespoons coarsely shredded mozzarella. Arrange the stir-fry mix on top, dividing equally, then sprinkle each with 1 more tablespoon mozzarella. Bake as directed in Step 4 and serve.

Little Pesto and Pignoli Loaves Prepare the basic recipe as directed through Step 2. Remove from the oven, spread each piece of baguette with 2 tablespoons of pesto sauce (homemade or bottled), sprinkle with 2 tablespoons coarsely shredded mozzarella, then 2 tablespoons coarsely chopped pine nuts, then 1 tablespoon coarsely grated Parmesan. Bake as directed in Step 4 and serve.

BLACK OLIVE FLAT BREAD WITH THYME

MAKES 6 TO 8 SERVINGS

Here's yet another quick loaf that begins with frozen yeast dough. This one's savory and good with almost anything Italian.

One 1-pound loaf frozen white bread dough, thawed and at room temperature

1/2 cup pitted, oil-cured ripe olives, quartered

1/2 teaspoon fresh lemon thyme leaves or 1/4 teaspoon crumbled dried leaf thyme

2 teaspoons olive oil

1/4 teaspoon kosher salt

1. Roll the dough on a lightly floured surface into a 15 × 10-inch rectangle. The dough will be elastic and keep pulling back, but persist and if necessary, let the dough rest 5 minutes to relax the gluten.

2. Scatter the olives and ¼ teaspoon of the fresh thyme (⅛ teaspoon of the dried) evenly over the surface of the dough, then roll up jelly-roll fashion forming a log 10 inches long.

3. Coat a baking sheet with nonstick cooking spray. Ease the roll of dough onto the sheet and flatten as much as possible. Brush with the olive oil, then sprinkle with the salt and remaining thyme. Cover loosely with wax paper and set in a warm, draft-free spot until the loaf begins to rise, about 30 minutes.

4. Toward the end of the rising, preheat the oven to 400°F. Bake the loaf on the middle oven shelf until nicely browned and hollow-sounding when thumped, 20 to 25 minutes.

5. Remove the loaf from the pan, easing onto a wire rack, and cool at least 15 minutes before cutting.

SEMOLINA-ROSEMARY-PARMESAN LOAF

MAKES 6 TO 8 SERVINGS

Like the yeast loaves that precede, this one begins with frozen dough. It's a particular favorite because I like the combination of semolina, freshly grated Parmesan, and fresh rosemary. I grow gobs of it not only because I use a lot of it in cooking but also because its intense, resiny aroma deer-proofs my garden.

> **One 1-pound loaf frozen white bread dough, thawed and at room temperature**
> **¹/4 cup semolina**
> **¹/4 cup grated Parmesan (page 18)**
> **1 tablespoon coarsely chopped fresh rosemary**
> **2 teaspoons olive oil**

1. Roll the dough into a 15 × 10-inch rectangle on a surface dusted with 1 tablespoon of the semolina. The dough will be elastic and keep pulling back, but persist and if necessary, let the dough rest 5 minutes to relax the gluten.

2. Sprinkle the sheet of dough with 1 tablespoon each of the semolina and Parmesan, and 1 teaspoon of the rosemary. Fold the dough in thirds just as you would when folding a letter, forming a 10 × 5-inch rectangle. Bearing down hard, roll the dough into a 12 × 8-inch rectangle. Sprinkle with another 1 tablespoon each of the semolina and Parmesan, and 1 teaspoon of rosemary. Fold in thirds to make an 8 × 4-inch loaf.

3. Coat a baking sheet with nonstick cooking spray. Ease the loaf onto the sheet and flatten as much as possible. Brush with olive oil and sprinkle with the remaining semolina, Parmesan, and rosemary. Cover loosely with wax paper and set in a warm, draft-free spot until the loaf begins to rise, about 30 minutes.

4. Toward the end of the rising, preheat the oven to 400°F. Bake the loaf on the middle oven shelf until nicely browned and hollow-sounding when thumped, 20 to 25 minutes.

5. Remove the loaf from the pan, easing onto a wire rack, and cool at least 15 minutes before cutting.

HERB-PARMESAN BUBBLE LOAF

MAKES 6 TO 8 SERVINGS

This savory variation of monkey bread shouldn't be sliced. Instead, pass the warm loaf and let everyone have fun pulling it apart. The only time-consuming part of the recipe is waiting for the dough to rise. At least you don't have to minister to the dough and can be off about your business.

> **One 1-pound loaf frozen bread dough**
> **1/4 cup olive oil**
> **1/2 cup grated Parmesan (page 18)**
> **1/4 cup fine dry bread crumbs**
> **1/2 teaspoon Basic Herb Mix (page 15)**
> **1/4 teaspoon freshly ground black pepper**

1. Thaw the frozen dough just until you can cut it, about 30 minutes. Meanwhile, line a 9 × 5 × 3-inch loaf pan with aluminum foil, placing the shiny side against the pan and leaving a 1-inch overhang all around; lightly grease the foil with vegetable oil.

2. Pour the olive oil into a small bowl and set aside. Place the Parmesan, bread crumbs, herb mix, and pepper in a plastic bag and shake to combine.

3. Cut the slightly thawed dough crosswise into 8 slices, then quarter each slice. Roll the chunks of dough into free-form balls. Working with several at a time, roll the dough balls in the oil, then shake in the Parmesan mixture until nicely coated.

4. Arrange the balls randomly in the pan. Cover loosely with wax paper and set in a warm, draft-free spot until the dough has risen by 50 percent, 2 to 2½ hours. Toward the end of rising, preheat the oven to 400°F.

5. Bake the bread on the middle oven shelf until richly browned and hollow-sounding when thumped, 20 to 25 minutes. Cool the bread in the upright pan on a wire rack for 15 minutes.

6. Lift the bread from the pan using the foil; loosen the sides of the bread from the foil and carefully pull the foil from beneath the loaf. Ease the loaf onto a bread board or into a basket and serve warm.

MORAVIAN SUGAR CAKE

MAKES 6 TO 8 SERVINGS

True Moravian Sugar Cake is made from yeast dough as rich as brioche. My quick version is crisp-crusted, like pizza. But it's dimpled the old-timey way and strewn with butter, brown sugar, and cinnamon. Let the kids do the dimpling and strewing—it's more fun than Play-Doh.

> **One 1-pound loaf frozen white bread dough, thawed and at room temperature**
> **3 tablespoons melted butter**
> **2 tablespoons packed light brown sugar**
> **1/2 teaspoon ground cinnamon**

1. Lightly coat a 13 × 9 × 2-inch baking pan with nonstick cooking spray and set aside.
2. Roll the thawed dough on a lightly floured surface to fit the pan. The dough will be quite elastic and keep springing back, but persist and, if necessary, let the dough rest about 5 minutes to relax the gluten.
3. Fit the dough into the pan, cover loosely with a clean dry cloth, and set in a warm spot, away from drafts, until it begins to rise, about 30 minutes. Meanwhile, combine the butter and brown sugar.
4. Toward the end of the rising period, preheat the oven to 400°F. Dimple the dough all over with your fingers, then fill the dimples with bits of the brown sugar mixture. Using a small, fine-mesh sieve, dust the top with the cinnamon.
5. Bake the sugar cake on the middle oven shelf until richly browned and hollow-sounding when thumped, 15 to 20 minutes.
6. Cool the sugar cake slightly in the pan on a wire rack, then cut into rectangles and serve.

ON MY FIRST KITCHEN SOLO—I couldn't have been more than four—I nearly burned the house down. All because I liked to cook on fast-forward.

The recipe I made that fateful day was my grandmother's soft ginger cake. Mother and I measured the ingredients (I hadn't yet learned to read), lined them up in the order that they were to be used, set the oven temperature and timer. Then Mother, brave soul, went out into the yard with my father so that I could make that cake all by myself.

Even then I reasoned that if I spooned the batter into muffin tins, the cake would bake faster than in a single large loaf pan. I also figured that if I revved up the oven temperature, it would bake faster still. So I shoved the thermostat up as far as it would go (to "broil," it turns out), slid the muffin pans into the oven, and trotted out to play. Soon smoke was billowing out of the kitchen window and my parents came running. I wasn't spanked that day but I was banned from the kitchen until I learned to follow directions.

I never did fully learn, which is why I continue to experiment. Especially when it comes to streamlining

CAKES, PUDDING LOAVES, *and* OTHER DESSERTS

cake-making methods. Throughout my growing-up years, I played around with "dump" cakes, making them always from scratch. I did try a couple of commercial cake mixes but never found them to be as good as what I could make myself.

All of the cakes in this chapter are quick from-scratch cakes and most of them begin with one of my homemade mixes. Keep these in fridge or freezer, then dip in whenever you yearn for a fresh-baked cake—almost any kind of cake because these mixes are amazingly versatile.

Cakes aren't the whole story here, however. I also include some heavenly pudding and ice cream loaves. For these are quick-to-mix, too.

SIMPLE YELLOW CAKE
WITH BROILED-ON BROWN SUGAR AND COCONUT

MAKES AN 8 X 8 X 2-INCH LOAF CAKE

My mother used to make this cake but she did it the old-fashioned way, creaming the butter and sugar, beating the eggs in one by one, then adding the sifted dry ingredients alternately with the milk. And to tell the truth, her cake wasn't as tender as my streamlined version.

CAKE

2^1/2 cups Quick Cake Mix (page 12)
^{1}/2 cup milk
2 large eggs
1^1/2 teaspoons vanilla extract

TOPPING

^{1}/3 cup packed light or dark brown sugar
3 tablespoons half-and-half
2 tablespoons melted butter
^{3}/4 cup sweetened flaked or shredded coconut

1. Preheat the oven to 375°F. Coat an 8 × 8 × 2-inch pan with nonstick cooking spray and set aside.
2. CAKE: Place the cake mix in a large bowl and make a well in the middle. Whisk the milk, eggs, and vanilla in a 1-quart measure until well blended, pour into the well, then fold in gently but completely using a large rubber spatula.
3. Scoop the batter into the pan, spreading to the corners, and bake in the lower third of the oven until lightly browned and a cake tester inserted in the middle of the cake comes out clean, 30 to 35 minutes.

4. TOPPING: While the cake bakes, whisk the brown sugar, half-and-half, and melted butter until smooth, add the coconut, and mix well. Set aside.

5. When the cake tests done, remove from the oven and preheat the broiler. Pour the coconut mixture on top of the cake and spread smoothly over the surface. Return to the oven, setting 4 to 5 inches from the broiler unit, and broil until the topping bubbles and browns lightly, 2 to 3 minutes.

6. Cool the cake in the pan on a wire rack to room temperature, cut into small squares, and serve.

LEMON VERBENA CAKE

MAKES A 9-INCH ROUND LOAF CAKE

Lemon verbena, one of the loveliest herbs, deserves to be better known. I've used it for years in fruit salads and sorbets, and as a garnish for all manner of desserts. Its flavor is not unlike that of lemongrass, only mellower somehow and more delicate. This time I wanted to season an easy yellow cake with lemon verbena. Would its delicate flavor be authoritative enough? Yes indeed. Would oven heat destroy its citrusy freshness? Or turn its basil-green leaves a dismal shade of brown? No, thank heavens, no. I grow gobs of lemon verbena in my herb garden (and I grew it for years on a sunny windowsill). If you have none on hand, the best place to find lemon verbena would be a farmers' market.

3 cups Quick Cake Mix (page 12)
$1/8$ teaspoon baking soda
$1/2$ cup milk
$1/3$ cup finely chopped tender young lemon verbena leaves
    (you'll need about 2 cups leaves—do not pack them in
    the measure)
2 large eggs
2 tablespoons fresh lemon juice
1 tablespoon confectioners' (10X) sugar

1. Preheat the oven to 375°F. Coat a 9-inch round layer cake pan with nonstick cooking spray and set aside.
2. Using your hands, toss the cake mix and soda in a large bowl until thoroughly combined, then make a well in the middle.
3. Whisk the milk, lemon verbena, eggs, and lemon juice in a 1-quart measure until well blended, pour into the well in the dry ingredients, then fold in gently but completely using a large rubber spatula. The batter will be very thick.

4. Scoop the batter into the pan, spreading to the edge, and bake in the lower third of the oven until lightly browned and a cake tester inserted in the middle of the cake comes out clean, 30 to 35 minutes.

5. Cool the cake in the upright pan on a wire rack 15 minutes, loosen around the edge with a thin-blade metal spatula, and invert the cake on a wire rack. Turn the cake right-side-up and cool on the rack to room temperature.

6. Just before serving, sift the confectioners' sugar over the top of the cake—through a lacy doily for a prettier presentation. Cut into slim wedges and serve.

INVERNESS SHORTBREAD

MAKES A 9-INCH ROUND SHORTBREAD

Scottish cooks press designs into their shortbreads using especially made wooden molds. I prick and score the top of mine—not as camera-ready but equally delicious. The keys to truly "short" shortbread are using a combination of wheat and rice or corn flour (cornstarch) and not overmixing once the flour goes in. This a recipe I picked up years ago while on assignment in the north of Scotland just above Loch Ness.

1 cup (2 sticks) butter, cut into pats, at room temperature
$2/3$ cup sugar
1 teaspoon vanilla extract
$1/8$ teaspoon salt
$1^1/2$ cups sifted all-purpose flour
$1/2$ cup sifted cornstarch

1. Preheat the oven to 375°F.
2. Cream the butter, sugar, vanilla, and salt at high electric mixer speed 4 to 5 minutes until fluffy and no sugar grains are discernible. Stop the mixer and scrape the bowl 2 or 3 times as you cream.
3. Sift the flour and cornstarch together onto a piece of wax paper. With the mixer set at low speed, add the flour mixture, about one-quarter of the total amount at a time, and beat after each addition only enough to combine.
4. Scoop the dough onto an ungreased rimmed baking sheet and then using a large rubber spatula, spread into a circle about 9 inches across and ½ inch thick. Smooth the top and prick lightly all over with a fork.
5. Bake the shortbread on the middle oven shelf for 5 minutes, reduce the oven temperature to 300°F, and continue baking until uniformly pale tan (slightly darker than a manilla folder) and soft to the touch, 35 to 40 minutes longer.

6. Remove from the oven, slide the baking sheet onto a wire rack, and cool the shortbread 5 minutes. Using a large sharp knife, mark 16 slim wedges in the top of the shortbread—it's easy if you rest a long ruler on the rim of the pan. First score the shortbread in quarters, then 8ths, then 16ths. Cool the shortbread to room temperature, break the wedges apart, and serve.

NOTE: *Stored in an airtight cannister in a cool, dry spot, this shortbread will keep fresh for at least 10 days.*

BARNSTABLE CRANBERRY SHORTBREAD WITH TOASTED PECANS

MAKES A 9-INCH ROUND LOAF

For special occasions, my niece Linda likes to bake this colorful shortbread. The recipe comes from her friend Laura Frost, for years the chef at a good little restaurant in Southern Pines, North Carolina. Alas, both have now moved south (Laura, literally, thus her restaurant is no more). This is my quicker, easier version. To toast the pecans, spread them on a small baking sheet and set in a 350°F oven for eight to ten minutes. Even easier, let the nuts toast while the oven preheats. But do watch closely lest they burn. When serving, cut the pieces small—this dessert is RICH.

2 cups fresh or frozen cranberries (do not thaw)

2 large Gala or Golden Delicious apples, peeled, cored, and cut into 1/2-inch chunks

3/4 cup sugar blended with 2 tablespoons all-purpose flour

3/4 cup lightly toasted, coarsely chopped pecans (see headnote)

2 1/2 cups Quick Cake Mix (page 12)

1/2 cup (1 stick) butter, melted

2 large eggs, at room temperature

1 teaspoon finely grated orange or lemon zest

1 teaspoon vanilla extract

1. Preheat the oven to 350°F. Coat a 9-inch springform pan well with nonstick cooking spray and set aside.
2. Place the cranberries, apples, sugar mixture, and pecans in a large mixing bowl and toss well. Transfer to the springform pan, spreading evenly over the bottom.

3. Quickly wipe the mixing bowl dry, add the cake mix, and make a well in the center. Whisk the melted butter, eggs, orange zest, and vanilla in a 1-quart measure until well blended, pour into the well in the cake mix, then using a large rubber spatula, fold in gently but completely. Do not beat or you'll toughen the shortbread.

4. Scoop the batter over the cranberry mixture, spreading to the edge and smoothing the top.

5. Bake in the lower third of the oven until the shortbread is lightly browned and a cake tester inserted into the middle comes out clean, 45 to 50 minutes.

6. Cool the shortbread in the upright pan on a wire rack to room temperature. Release and remove the springform sides but do not remove the pan bottom. Instead, slide the shortbread, pan bottom and all, onto a round platter. Cut into slim wedges and serve as is or, if you prefer, topped with whipped cream or vanilla ice cream.

ORANGE MARMALADE CAKE

For best results, use a bright orange marmalade that isn't too thick. Because of its richness, this cake falls ever so slightly on cooling but its texture is lovely and light.

> **2 cups Quick Cake Mix (page 12)**
> **1/2 teaspoon baking soda**
> **1 cup pecans, coarsely chopped**
> **1/2 cup orange marmalade (see headnote)**
> **1/2 cup orange juice**
> **2 tablespoons Grand Marnier or 1 teaspoon orange extract**
> **1 teaspoon vanilla extract**
> **1 extra-large egg**

1. Preheat the oven to 375°F. Coat an 8 × 8 × 2-inch pan with nonstick cooking spray and set aside.
2. Whisk the cake mix and soda in a large bowl until combined. Add ½ cup of the pecans and toss well. Make a well in the middle of the dry ingredients.
3. Whisk the marmalade, orange juice, Grand Marnier, and vanilla in a 1-quart measure until smooth. Add the egg and whisk quickly to combine. Pour into the well in the dry ingredients and gently fold in using a large rubber spatula. Don't beat. The batter should be lumpy and it's good if a few floury streaks show.
4. Scoop the batter into the pan, spreading to the corners, and scatter the remaining ½ cup pecans evenly on top. Bake in the lower third of the oven until richly browned and a cake tester inserted in the middle of the loaf comes out clean, 30 to 35 minutes.
5. Cool the loaf in the pan on a wire rack to room temperature, cut into squares, and serve.

GREEN TOMATO UPSIDE-DOWN CAKE

MAKES A 10-INCH ROUND CAKE

Apart from frying green tomatoes, this is my favorite way to prepare them. They add a lemony counterpoint to the sweetness of the cake and I find their design more appealing than the proverbial pineapple rings.

> 3 tablespoons butter
>
> 1/4 cup packed light brown sugar
>
> 1 1/4 teaspoons Three-Spice Mix (page 13)
>
> 1 large, hard green tomato (6 to 8 ounces), cored and sliced
>   1/4-inch thick
>
> 2 1/2 cups Quick Cake Mix (page 12)
>
> 1/2 cup milk
>
> 2 large eggs
>
> 2 tablespoons molasses (not too dark)
>
> 1 teaspoon vanilla extract

1. Coat the bottom (but not the sides) of a well-seasoned 10-inch cast-iron skillet with nonstick cooking spray. Add the butter, set on a rack in the lower third of the oven, and preheat the oven to 350°F.
2. Remove the skillet from the oven, blend the brown sugar and ¼ teaspoon of the spice mix into the melted butter, then spread evenly over the bottom of the skillet. Arrange the tomato slices in a decorative pattern in the brown sugar mixture, cutting as needed to fit. Spray a crumple of paper toweling with nonstick cooking spray and rub over the sides of the skillet. Set the skillet aside.
3. Whisk the cake mix and remaining spice mix in a large bowl until combined. Make a well in the middle of the dry ingredients.

4. Whisk the milk, eggs, molasses, and vanilla in a 1-quart measure until well blended, pour into the well in the dry ingredients, and fold in gently but completely using a large rubber spatula. Don't beat—the batter should be lumpy.

5. Scoop the batter into the skillet, spreading to the edge, and bake in the lower third of the oven until lightly browned and a cake tester inserted in the middle of the cake comes out clean, 30 to 35 minutes.

6. Cool the cake in the upright skillet on a wire rack 5 minutes. Loosen the cake around the edge, then invert on a colorful round platter. Instead of removing the inverted skillet at once, let it stand a minute or two, then carefully lift it off. If any tomato slices have stuck to the bottom of the skillet, simply set them back on the cake—no one will be the wiser.

7. To serve, cut the cake into wedges, making sure that each person gets some green tomato.

SHENANDOAH BLACKBERRY CAKE
WITH BROWNED BUTTER FROSTING

MAKES A 13 X 9 X 2-INCH LOAF CAKE

Summertime in the Blue Ridge and broad Shenandoah Valley means wild blackberries and dodging thorns and brambles to pick them. But the rewards are huge—fresh-baked blackberry pies and cobblers, homemade jams, jellies, and preserves, and not least, this unusual blackberry cake made from those preserves. For best results, use smooth preserves instead of lumpy because large bits of berry will sink to the bottom of the batter. I find this cake perfect for picnics because it can be made ahead, it travels well, and feeds an army.

CAKE

3 cups Quick Bread Mix (page 9)

$3/4$ cup sugar

1 tablespoon Three-Spice Mix (page 13)

$1/2$ teaspoon baking soda

$3/4$ cup buttermilk

$3/4$ cup packed blackberry preserves (see headnote)

3 large eggs

1 teaspoon vanilla extract

FROSTING

3 tablespoons butter

$2^1/2$ cups unsifted confectioners' (10X) sugar

1 teaspoon vanilla extract

3 to 4 tablespoons milk or cream (half-and-half, light, or heavy)

1. Preheat the oven to 350°F. Coat a 13 × 9 × 2-inch pan with nonstick oil-and-flour baking spray and set aside.
2. CAKE: Whisk the bread mix, sugar, spice mix, and soda in a large bowl until combined, then make a well in the middle of the dry ingredients.
3. Whisk the buttermilk and blackberry preserves in a 2-quart measure until fairly smooth (lentil-size lumps are okay but nothing larger). Add the eggs and vanilla and whisk quickly to combine. Pour into the well in the dry ingredients and gently fold in using a large rubber spatula. Don't beat. The batter should be lumpy and it's good if a few floury streaks show.
4. Scoop the batter into the pan, spreading to the corners, and bake in the lower third of the oven until the cake begins to pull from the sides of the pan and a cake tester inserted in the middle comes out clean, about 30 minutes.
5. FROSTING: While the cake is in the oven, melt the butter in a butter warmer or very small heavy saucepan over low heat, then allow it to brown slowly until the color of amber—this will take 10 to 12 minutes. Pour into a ramekin and set in the refrigerator.
6. When the cake tests done, cool in the pan on a wire rack to room temperature.
7. To finish the frosting, cream the chilled butter, confectioners' sugar, and vanilla until smooth—I do this in a food processor fitted with the metal chopping blade. Then beat in the milk, tablespoon by tablespoon, until the frosting is good spreading consistency.
8. Swirl the frosting over the top of the cake, then allow to dry for about half an hour before cutting into squares. Make the pieces small—this cake is super-rich. Just the way Southerners like it.

BLUEBERRY CRUMB CAKE

MAKES AN 8 X 8 X 2-INCH LOAF CAKE

I'm almost embarassed to include this recipe because it's so, so easy. To make things even easier, you can substitute solidly frozen unsweetened blueberries for the fresh (no washing or stemming needed), but if you do, you must increase the baking time by ten to fifteen minutes. Also try the variations given at the end of the recipe. They're equally quick and delicious.

CAKE

> 2^{1}/2 cups Quick Cake Mix (page 12)
>
> 1 teaspoon Three-Spice Mix (page 13)
>
> ^{1}/2 cup milk
>
> 1 large egg
>
> 1 teaspoon vanilla extract

TOPPING

> 1^{1}/2 cups washed and stemmed fresh blueberries or
>
>   1^{1}/2 cups solidly frozen unsweetened blueberries
>
> ^{1}/2 cup Quick Cake Mix
>
> ^{1}/2 teaspoon Three-Spice Mix
>
> ^{1}/2 cup sliced almonds

1. Preheat the oven to 375°F. Coat an 8 × 8 × 2-inch pan with nonstick cooking spray and set aside.
2. CAKE: Whisk the cake and spice mixes together in a large bowl to combine, then make a well in the middle of the dry ingredients.

3. Whisk the milk, egg, and vanilla in a 1-quart measure until smooth. Pour into the well in the dry ingredients and gently fold in using a large rubber spatula. The batter should be lumpy with a few floury streaks clearly visible. Scoop the batter into the pan, spreading to the corners.

4. TOPPING: Scatter the blueberries evenly on top of the batter. Quickly whisk together the cake and spice mixes, add the sliced almonds, and toss well to dredge. Sprinkle over the blueberries, covering them entirely.

5. Bake the crumb cake in the lower third of the oven until richly browned and a cake tester thrust into the middle comes out clean—about 40 minutes if you use fresh blueberries, 50 to 55 if you use the solidly frozen.

6. Cool the loaf in the pan on a wire rack to room temperature, cut into squares, and serve as is or with whipped cream or vanilla ice cream scooped aboard.

VARIATION

Strawberry Crumb Cake Prepare the cake as directed but omit the spice mix and whisk 1 teaspoon finely grated orange zest along with the milk, egg, and vanilla. In the topping, substitute 1½ cups thinly sliced, hulled fresh strawberries for the blueberries. Proceed as directed, baking for about 40 minutes.

Apple or Pear Crumb Cake Prepare the cake as directed but whisk 1 teaspoon finely grated lemon zest and ¼ teaspoon almond extract along with the milk, egg, and vanilla. In the topping, substitute 1½ cups thinly sliced, cored, and peeled Golden Delicious apples, or Bosc or Bartlett pears for the blueberries (about 3 medium apples or pears). Also substitute ½ cup coarsely chopped pecans for the almonds. Proceed as directed, baking for about 40 minutes.

DRIED APPLE CAKE WITH CHOPPED PECANS

MAKES AN 9 X 9 X 2-INCH LOAF CAKE

My grocery only carries dried apple rings and they are leathery as all get-out. I've discovered, however, that if I freeze them, then break them apart, my food processor can chop them as coarse or fine as I like. For this recipe, they should be twice as coarse as oatmeal. But, make a note, your processor blade must be super-sharp and your machine a sturdy one that won't walk or stall. If you have no processor, the best alternative is to snip the apples with kitchen shears but this does take time and energy. My chef's knife was useless—couldn't make clean cuts. Moreover I was forever having to remove pieces of apple that had stuck to the blade. Hardly efficient. As for the pecans, processor-chop enough for both the cake and the frosting, then divide.

CAKE

3 cups Quick Cake Mix (page 12)

1^1/2 teaspoons Three-Spice Mix (page 13)

1 cup coarsely chopped pecans

1 cup coarsely chopped dried apples

^{3}/4 cup milk

2 large eggs

1 teaspoon vanilla extract

I teaspoon finely grated lemon zest

TOPPING

^{1}/2 cup coarsely chopped pecans

^{1}/3 cup Quick Cake Mix

3 tablespoons raw (turbinado) sugar or light brown sugar

^{1}/2 teaspoon Three-Spice Mix

1. Preheat the oven to 375°F. Coat a 9 × 9 × 2-inch pan with nonstick oil-and-flour baking spray and set aside.

2. CAKE: Whisk the cake and spice mixes in a large bowl until combined. Add the pecans and apples and toss until nicely dredged. Make a well in the middle of the dry ingredients.

3. Whisk the milk, eggs, vanilla, and lemon zest in a 2-quart measure until well blended, pour into the well in the dry ingredients, then fold in gently but completely using a large rubber spatula. Scoop the batter into the pan, spreading to the corners.

4. TOPPING: Quickly mix all ingredients together and scatter evenly over the top of the batter. Bake the cake in the lower third of the oven until lightly browned and a cake tester inserted in the middle comes out clean, 30 to 35 minutes.

5. Cool the cake in the pan on a wire rack to room temperature, cut into squares, and serve.

STRAWBERRY RIPPLE CAKE

MAKES AN 8 X 8 X 2-INCH LOAF CAKE

Almost any bright red fruit jam will do here—strawberry, raspberry, currant, cherry—but do choose one that's smooth and seedless. The easiest way to melt the jam is in a microwave oven: scoop the jam into a one-quart ovenproof glass measure, cover with wax paper, then microwave about two minutes on LOW. Once the jam is melted, whisk it until smooth, then keep it warm so that it's fluid when it goes on the cake batter.

2^1/2 cups Quick Cake Mix (page 12)

^{1}/2 cup milk

2 large eggs

1 tablespoon finely grated orange zest

1 teaspoon lemon extract

^{1}/3 cup firmly packed strawberry jam, melted (see headnote)

1. Preheat the oven to 350°F. Coat an 8 × 8 × 2-inch pan with nonstick oil-and-flour baking spray and set aside.
2. Place the cake mix in a large bowl and make a well in the middle. Whisk the milk, eggs, orange zest, and lemon extract in a 1-quart measure until well blended, pour into the well, then fold in gently but completely using a large rubber spatula.
3. Scoop the batter into the pan, spreading to the corners. Drop the melted jam on top of the batter from a tablespoon, making three rows of three (think tick-tack-toe). Insert a thin-blade metal spatula into the jam puddle in the upper left-hand corner, pushing it to the bottom of the pan, then draw it down through the first vertical row of jam puddles. Reverse direction, drawing the spatula through the

middle row of jam puddles, then reverse direction once again, drawing the spatula through the third row. Give the pan a one-quarter turn and repeat the process so that the batter is well marbled with jam.

4. Bake the cake in the lower third of the oven until lightly browned and a cake tester inserted in the middle comes out clean, 35 to 40 minutes.

5. Cool the cake in the pan on a wire rack to room temperature, cut into small squares, and serve.

BAVARIAN HAZELNUT TORTE

MAKES A 10-INCH, 2-LAYER CAKE

My German friend Hedy Würz often serves this flourless, four-ingredient cake at dinner parties and I like it so much it was the first recipe to go into our New German Cookbook (HarperCollins, 1993). The original recipe calls for raw hazelnuts, but I prefer the heightened flavor of toasted nuts (for toasting how-tos, see page 16 in the Basics chapter). To grind the hazelnuts, I use a food processor. The trick is to grind them until fine and feathery without reducing them to paste—no problem if you keep your eye on the machine and your finger on the pulse button.

> **10 extra-large eggs, separated**
> **1^1/$_2$ cups sugar**
> **4 cups finely ground lightly toasted hazelnuts (see headnote)**
> **1/4 teaspoon salt**
> **2^1/$_2$ cups ice-cold heavy cream whipped to stiff peaks with 3 tablespoons confectioners' (10X) sugar and 1 teaspoon vanilla extract (frosting and filling)**
> **12 lightly toasted whole hazelnuts with the skins rubbed off (decoration)**

1. Preheat the oven to 350°F. Generously coat two 10-inch springform pans with nonstick cooking spray, dust well with flour, tapping out the excess, and set the pans aside.
2. Beat the egg yolks and sugar in a bowl at highest electric mixer speed until as thick and pale as mayonnaise, about 5 minutes. With the machine set at low speed, mix in the hazelnuts—the batter will be very thick.

3. Whip the egg whites with the salt to stiff peaks, then fold one-quarter of them into the hazelnut mixture to lighten it. Next fold in the remaining whites until no streaks of white or brown remain—easy does it.

4. Divide the batter between the two pans, smooth the tops, and set in the lower third of the oven so that the pans do not touch one another or the oven walls. Bake until the torte layers are lightly browned and springy to the touch, about 45 minutes.

5. Cool the torte layers in the upright pans on wire racks 10 minutes, then loosen each around the edge with a thin-blade metal spatula. Release and remove the springform pan sides. Carefully separate the layers from the pan bottoms with the spatula, then lift to wire racks, and cool to room temperature.

6. Place one torte layer upside-down on a large round serving plate, spread thickly with the flavored whipped cream, then set the second layer on top, right-side-up. Swirl the remaining whipped cream over the top of the torte (but not the sides), then ring the whole toasted hazelnuts around the edge. Cut into wedges and serve—I like to do this at the table because the torte is so pretty. It's big enough, by the way, to serve a dozen people.

GLAMORGAN DATE-WALNUT CAKE

MAKES AN 8^{1}/$_{2}$ X 4^{1}/$_{2}$ X 2^{3}/$_{4}$-INCH LOAF CAKE

Years ago when I was traveling about Wales on assignment, my hostess at a farmhouse bed-and-breakfast where I was staying served this simple cake at afternoon tea. I liked it so much she gave me her handwritten recipe, which I've streamlined by using my Quick Bread Mix and the chopped dates now carried by most supermarkets. The only spice in the recipe is nutmeg (a particular Welsh favorite) and it should be freshly grated—the microplane does the job in seconds.

2^{1}/$_{2}$ cups Quick Bread Mix (page 9)

^{1}/$_{2}$ cup packed dark brown sugar

^{1}/$_{2}$ teaspoon freshly grated nutmeg

1 cup coarsely chopped walnuts

1 cup coarsely chopped pitted dates (see headnote)

^{1}/$_{2}$ cup milk

2 large eggs

1. Preheat the oven to 375°F. Coat an 8^{1}/$_{2}$ × 4^{1}/$_{2}$ × 2^{3}/$_{4}$-inch pan with nonstick oil-and-flour baking spray, then set aside.
2. Place the bread mix, brown sugar, and nutmeg in a large mixing bowl and toss well with your hands, pressing out any lumps of sugar. Add the walnuts and dates and toss until nicely dredged. Make a well in the middle of the dry ingredients.
3. Whisk the milk and eggs in a 1-quart measure until well blended. Pour into the well in the dry ingredients, then fold in using a large rubber spatula to form a biscuit-stiff dough—it's good if a few floury specks still show.
4. Scoop the dough into the pan, spreading to the corners, and bake in the lower third of the oven until nicely browned and a cake tester inserted in the middle of the cake comes out clean, 45 to 50 minutes.

5. Cool the loaf in the upright pan on a wire rack 15 minutes, then loosen around the edge and invert on the rack. Turn right-side-up and cool to room temperature before slicing.

Date-Pecan Cake Prepare as directed substituting light brown sugar for dark and pecans (or black walnuts) for the walnuts. In Step 3, whisk 1 tablespoon vanilla extract along with the milk and eggs, then proceed as the recipe directs.

CARROT CAKE

I never frost carrot cake—who needs the extra calories? This cake, moreover, is so moist, so rich that adding an icing—even a skim-coat—is lily-gilding. To speed preparation, I use my trusty food processor to chop the pecans, grate the orange zest, reduce the shredded carrots from the produce section to manageable size, combine the dry ingredients, and finally, the liquids. The key in using a food processor is to begin with the dry ingredients and end with the wet so that you don't have to stop to wash, rinse, or wipe the bowl and blade between steps. This cake can of course be made entirely by hand—see the variation at the end for the changes in sequence.

1 1/2 cups pecans

1 1/4 cups packed dark brown sugar

Four 3-inch strips orange zest (I just run a vegetable peeler
    the length of the orange)

3 cups sifted self-rising all-purpose flour

2 teaspoons Five-Spice Mix (page 14)

1/4 teaspoon baking soda

One 10-ounce package (4 cups) coarsely shredded carrots

3/4 cup vegetable oil

3/4 cup buttermilk

3 large eggs

1 tablespoon vanilla extract

1. Preheat the oven to 375°F. Coat a 10 × 5 × 4-inch pan with nonstick oil-and-flour baking spray and set aside.

2. Coarsely chop the pecans in a food processor fitted with the metal chopping blade by pulsing briskly—6 to 8 times should do it. Tip into a large mixing bowl. Add the sugar and orange zest to the processor and churn for about a minute or until the orange zest is finely grated; scrape the work bowl at halftime. Add the flour, spice mix, and soda and pulse quickly to combine. Add to the nuts and toss well. Make a well in the middle of the dry ingredients.

3. Add the carrots to the machine and chop moderately fine using 4 to 5 long pulses. Add the oil, buttermilk, eggs, and vanilla and pulse quickly to combine. Pour into the well in the dry ingredients, then fold in using a large rubber spatula to form a stiff batter with a few floury specks still visible.

4. Scoop the batter into the pan, spreading to the corners, and bake in the lower third of the oven until nicely browned and a cake tester stuck into the middle of the cake comes out clean, about 1 hour and 10 minutes.

5. Cool the loaf in the upright pan on a wire rack 15 minutes, then loosen around the edge and invert on the rack. Turn right-side-up and cool to room temperature before slicing.

TO MAKE THIS CAKE BY HAND

1. Place the sugar, flour, spice mix, and soda in a large mixing bowl and mix well with your hands, pressing out any lumps of sugar. Coarsely chop the pecans, add them to the bowl, and toss well to dredge; make a well in the middle of the dry ingredients.

2. Instead of adding strips of orange zest, use a microplane to finely grate 1 tablespoon of zest. Combine the vegetable oil, buttermilk, eggs, vanilla, and grated orange zest in a 2-quart measure by whisking hard. Chop the carrot shreds fairly fine, and whisk them into the liquids. Pour into the well in the dry ingredients, pick up at this point in Step 3, and proceed as the recipe directs.

HUMMINGBIRD LOAF
WITH SOUR CREAM–PECAN FROSTING

MAKES A 13 X 9 X 2-INCH LOAF CAKE

I have no idea when or where this cake originated but I do know that it's a favorite Down South. Its name is said to come from the fact that once you eat it, you'll hum with joy. Classic Hummingbird Cake is a three-layer affair sandwiched together with heavy cream cheese frosting. I've simplified things by turning this into a less labor-intensive loaf cake. I've also lightened the frosting by using sour cream instead of cream cheese. Some Hummingbird Cakes call for coconut, others don't, and I quite frankly find the cake rich enough without the added calories and saturated fat. Most Southerners use pecans in this recipe but you can substitute wild hickory nuts (a type of pecan), black walnuts, or English walnuts. Because the cake and frosting both call for nuts, I chop the lot in the food processor, then divide.

In fact, I make the cake almost entirely by food processor because it's so quick. If you prefer doing things by hand, simply combine all dry ingredients in a large bowl, add the nuts, toss well to dredge, then make a well in the middle of the "dries." Next, combine all of the wet ingredients, pour into the well in the dries, and fold in using a large rubber spatula. Do not beat the batter at any time because you will surely toughen your cake. Also, don't be alarmed by the number of ingredients here—this cake is quick.

CAKE

2 cups pecans

3 cups unsifted all-purpose flour (whisk lightly before measuring)

2 cups sugar

2 teaspoons Three-Spice Mix (page 13)

1 teaspoon baking soda

$^1/_2$ teaspoon salt

3 very ripe medium bananas (about 1 pound), peeled and cut
into 1-inch chunks (I cut the bananas directly into the
processor work bowl)

$1^1/_2$ cups vegetable oil

3 large eggs

2 teaspoons vanilla extract

One 8-ounce can crushed pineapple packed in juice (do not
drain)

FROSTING

$2^1/_2$ cups unsifted confectioners' (10 X) sugar

$^1/_4$ cup "light" sour cream (measure firmly packed)

1 teaspoon vanilla extract

1 to 3 teaspoons water (as needed for good spreading
consistency)

1 cup coarsely chopped pecans (reserved in Step 2)

1. Preheat the oven to 350° F. Coat a 13 × 9 × 2-inch baking pan with nonstick oil-
and-flour baking spray, then set aside.

2. CAKE: Pulse the pecans quickly in a food processor fitted with the metal chopping blade until coarsely chopped—8 to 10 zaps should do it. Place 1 cup of the chopped pecans in a large bowl and reserve the remaining 1 cup for the frosting.

3. Whiz the flour, sugar, spice mix, soda, and salt briefly in the processor to combine (no need to wash or wipe the work bowl or blade). Tip into the bowl with the pecans, toss until nicely dredged, then make a well in the middle of the dry ingredients.

4. Add the bananas to the processor (again, no need to wash or wipe) and churn 8 to 10 seconds. Scrape the work bowl, stir, and pulse out any largish lumps. Add the vegetable oil, eggs, and vanilla, and pulse quickly to combine. Add the pineapple and again pulse to combine. Pour the banana mixture into the well in the dry ingredients and fold in using a large rubber spatula—do not beat. In fact, it's best if a few floury streaks show.

5. Scoop the batter into the pan, spreading to the corners, and bake in the lower third of the oven until richly browned and a cake tester inserted in the middle of the cake comes out clean, about 45 minutes. Remove the cake from the oven and cool in the upright pan on a wire rack to room temperature.

6. FROSTING: Either by food processor or by hand, beat the confectioners' sugar, sour cream, and vanilla until smooth, then add just enough water—teaspoon by teaspoon—until the frosting can be spread. Fold in the 1 cup reserved chopped pecans.

7. Drop the frosting in clumps on top of the cooled cake, then spread evenly. This will be a thin layer of frosting—quite enough for this rich cake. Let the frosting harden for about half an hour, then cut the cake into small squares, and enjoy.

SWEET POTATO CAKE
WITH WILD HICKORY NUTS AND RAISINS

MAKES AN 8¹/₂ X 4¹/₂ X 2³/₄-INCH LOAF CAKE

When I was little, we had a giant shagbark hickory tree in our front yard and after first frost, it rained nuts upon the ground. My job was to gather them, crack them, and extract the nuts, which were as sweet as pecans (a close relative). Not an easy job. I try to use wild hickory nuts here because they remind me of the sweet potato cake my mother used to bake. But if they are nowhere to be found, I substitute pecans, walnuts, even black walnuts. Like my mother, I usually make sweet potato cake when I have leftover sweet potato, but sometimes I'll bake a large one just for the cake (an hour at 400°F is all it takes).

NOTE: *Because sweet potatoes absorb and hold moisture, this cake takes more than an hour to bake. You can trim the oven time by about fifteen minutes if you use a 9 × 5 × 3-inch pan or by about half an hour if you use a 9 × 9 × 2-inch pan. But you won't have as full or high-rising a cake.*

> 2¹/₂ cups Quick Cake Mix (page 12)
> 1 tablespoon Three-Spice Mix (page 13)
> 1 cup coarsely chopped wild hickory nuts, pecans, walnuts,
>   or black walnuts
> ³/₄ cup seedless raisins
> ³/₄ cup packed leftover unseasoned mashed sweet potato
> ¹/₂ cup milk
> 2 large eggs
> 1 tablespoon vanilla extract

1. Preheat the oven to 375°F. Coat an 8¹/₂ × 4¹/₂ × 2³/₄-inch pan with nonstick oil-and-flour baking spray, then set aside.

2. Whisk the cake and spice mixes in a large mixing bowl to combine. Add the nuts and raisins and toss until nicely dredged. Make a well in the middle of the dry ingredients.

3. Whisk the sweet potato, milk, eggs, and vanilla in a 2-quart measure until well blended. Pour into the well in the dry ingredients, then fold in using a large rubber spatula to form a stiff batter—it's good if a few floury streaks show.

4. Scoop the batter into the pan, spreading to the corners, and bake in the lower third of the oven until richly browned and a cake tester inserted in the middle of the cake comes out clean—1 hour and 10 to 15 minutes.

5. Cool the cake in the upright pan on a wire rack 15 minutes, then loosen around the edge and invert on the rack. Turn right-side-up and cool to room temperature before slicing.

PINEAPPLE-MACADAMIA CAKE

MAKES AN 8 X 8 X 2-INCH LOAF CAKE

All the flavors of Hawaii in a zip-quick cake. Raw sugar adds a slightly caramel taste suggestive of roasted pineapple. Most supermarkets now carry it but if you're unable to find it, substitute granulated sugar or, if you prefer, a 50-50 mix of granulated and light brown sugar.

> 2 cups Quick Bread Mix (page 9)
> $2/3$ cup raw (turbinado) sugar
> 2 teaspoons Three-Spice Mix (page 13)
> $1/2$ teaspoon baking soda
> 1 cup coarsely chopped macadamia nuts
> One 8-ounce can crushed pineapple, very well drained and
>   2 tablespoons juice reserved
> 2 large eggs
> 1 teaspoon vanilla extract

1. Preheat the oven to 375°F. Coat an 8 × 8 × 2-inch baking pan with nonstick cooking spray and set aside.
2. Whisk the bread mix, sugar, spice mix, and baking soda together in a large bowl until well blended. Add the macadamias and toss well. Make a well in the middle of the dry ingredients.
3. Whisk the pineapple with the reserved juice, eggs, and vanilla in a 1-quart measure to combine. Pour into the well in the dry ingredients, then using a large rubber spatula, fold in just until the batter is uniformly moist but still lumpy—do not beat.
4. Scoop the batter into the pan, spreading to the corners, and bake in the lower third of the oven until nicely browned and a cake tester inserted in the middle of the cake comes out clean, 30 to 35 minutes.
5. Cool the cake in the upright pan on a wire rack to room temperature, then cut into large squares and serve.

PRUNE CAKE WITH COFFEE FROSTING

MAKES A 9 X 9 X 2-INCH LOAF CAKE

Fresh out of Cornell, I went to work for the North Carolina Agricultural Extension Service as an assistant home demonstration agent in Iredell County, a hundred and fifty miles west of Raleigh where I'd grown up. Every August—night after night—gargantuan home demonstration club picnics were spread on plank-and-sawhorse tables under sheltering oaks. With thirty-something clubs in the county, there was a picnic every night, sometimes two the same night, and I usually went to them all. You have never seen such glorious food, almost all of it made from old family recipes. It didn't take me long to learn which club women were the ace bakers and whenever this prune cake appeared, I'd snatch a piece first thing knowing that it would disappear in no time.

Here's a quick and easy version that takes advantage of a fairly new supermarket staple: pitted, bite-size prunes (now also called "dried plums"). For this recipe, you'll need three-quarters cup of prune purée—easy enough thanks to the microwave oven and the food processor. To make the purée: place one cup of pitted bite-size prunes in a two-quart ovenproof glass measure, add one-half cup water, cover with wax paper, and microwave on HIGH for five minutes, or about three minutes if you have one of the newer high-wattage microwave ovens. Let stand five minutes, then purée by churning in a food processor, either a mini or a full-size one. You should have exactly the amount of prune purée that you need.

CAKE

3 cups Quick Cake Mix (page 12)

2 teaspoons Five-Spice Mix (page 14)

1/4 teaspoon baking soda

1 cup coarsely chopped pecans, walnuts, or black walnuts

3/4 cup buttermilk

3/4 cup prune purée (see headnote)

2 large eggs

1 teaspoon vanilla extract

FROSTING

2 cups unsifted confectioners' (10X) sugar

2 tablespoons butter, at room temperature

1 teaspoon instant coffee crystals (preferably espresso)

1 teaspoon vanilla extract

2 to 3 tablespoons heavy cream or half-and-half

1. Preheat the oven to 375°F. Coat a 9 × 9 × 2-inch pan with nonstick oil-and-flour baking spray and set aside.

2. CAKE: Whisk the cake and spice mixes and soda together in a large bowl to combine. Add the pecans and toss until nicely dredged, then make a well in the middle of the dry ingredients.

3. Whisk the buttermilk, prune purée, eggs, and vanilla in a 2-quart measure until smooth. Pour into the well in the dry ingredients and gently fold in using a large rubber spatula. The batter should be lumpy with a few floury streaks clearly visible. Scoop the batter into the pan, spreading to the corners.

4. Bake in the lower third of the oven until lightly browned and a cake tester inserted into the middle of the cake comes out clean, 30 to 35 minutes. Remove the cake from the oven and cool in the pan on a wire rack to room temperature.

5. **FROSTING**: While the cake is cooling, use a hand electric mixer to beat the confectioners' sugar, butter, coffee crystals, and vanilla together in a small bowl until crumbly. Next beat in just enough cream to make the frosting a good spreading consistency. (I do this in the food processor, first pulsing the sugar, butter, coffee crystals, and vanilla together, then with the machine running, adding the cream tablespoon by tablespoon down the feed tube until I get exactly the right consistency.)

6. Swirl the frosting over the top of the cake in a thin layer. Allow the frosting to dry for about 30 minutes, then cut the cake into small squares and serve.

NOTE: *This coffee frosting is equally delicious spread over the top of any chocolate cake.*

BOURBON–PECAN PRALINE CAKE

MAKES AN 8 X 8 X 2-INCH LOAF CAKE

Mix the topping first so that it's ready to sprinkle over the batter. As the cake bakes, the brown sugar in the topping turns crunchy and the pecans toast lightly. I favor a silvery pan for this particular cake because a dark one may cause it to overbrown around the edge and on the bottom.

    TIP: *Chop all of the pecans together—1 cup total—then divide ¼ cup for the topping and ¾ cup for the cake.*

TOPPING

    1/4 cup firmly packed dark brown sugar

    1/4 cup coarsely chopped pecans

CAKE

    2 cups Quick Bread Mix (page 9)

    1/2 teaspoon baking soda

    3/4 cup firmly packed dark brown sugar

    3/4 cup coarsely chopped pecans

    3/4 cup buttermilk

    2 tablespoons bourbon

    2 teaspoons vanilla extract

    1 extra-large egg

1. Preheat the oven to 375°F. Coat an 8 × 8 × 2-inch pan with nonstick cooking spray and set aside.
2. TOPPING: Crumble the brown sugar into a small bowl, add the pecans and work the two together with your fingers until uniformly coarse. Set aside.

3. CAKE: Whisk the bread mix and soda in a large bowl until combined. Add the brown sugar and work it with your fingers. Add the pecans and toss well. Make a well in the middle of the dry ingredients.

4. Whisk the buttermilk, bourbon, vanilla, and egg in a 1-quart measure until smooth. Pour into the well in the dry ingredients and gently fold in using a large rubber spatula. The batter should be lumpy with a few floury streaks clearly visible.

5. Scoop the batter into the pan, spreading to the corners, and scatter the topping evenly over all. Bake in the lower third of the oven until richly browned and a cake tester inserted in the middle of the loaf comes out clean, 30 to 35 minutes.

6. Cool the loaf in the pan on a wire rack to room temperature, cut into squares, and serve.

PORT WINE CAKE WITH TOASTED ALMONDS

MAKES AN 8¹/2 X 4¹/2 X 2³/4-INCH LOAF CAKE

The Portuguese like to serve a fine port with cake and sometimes with toasted home-grown almonds as well. I've combined all three in this easy loaf cake. To toast the almonds, I give them eight to ten minutes in a 375°F oven, stirring well at halftime. They should be the color of old ivory. To chop them, I pulse several times in the food processor. That's all there is to it.

2¹/2 cups Quick Cake Mix (page 12)
¹/2 teaspoon Three-Spice Mix (page 13)
Two 2.25-ounce packages (1 cup) sliced almonds, lightly
    toasted and moderately finely chopped (see headnote)
¹/3 cup milk
¹/3 cup ruby port or other sweet wine
2 large eggs

1. Preheat the oven to 375°F. Coat an 8½ × 4½ × 2¾-inch pan with nonstick oil-and-flour baking spray, then set aside.
2. Whisk the cake and spice mixes together in a large mixing bowl to combine. Add the toasted almonds and toss to dredge. Make a well in the middle of the dry ingredients.
3. Whisk the milk, wine, and eggs in a 1-quart measure until well blended. Pour into the well in the dry ingredients, then fold in using a large rubber spatula. The batter should be stiff and lumpy with a few floury specks showing.
4. Scoop the batter into the pan, spreading to the corners, and bake in the lower third of the oven until nicely browned and a cake tester inserted in the middle of the cake comes out clean, 50 to 55 minutes.
5. Cool the loaf in the upright pan on a wire rack 10 minutes, then loosen around the edge and invert on the rack. Turn right-side-up and cool to room temperature before slicing.

OLD NORTH CAROLINA BUTTERMILK SPICE CAKE

MAKES AN 8 X 8 X 2-INCH LOAF CAKE

Back when I was in grammar school—pre-prefabbed food—there were wonderful cooks in the cafeteria kitchen who actually prepared everything we ate. Most Thursdays this spice cake—or one of its variations—was on the menu and I always grabbed a piece before it sold out. Here's a quick and easy version together with four equally fast variations.

$2^1/2$ cups Quick Bread Mix (page 9)

1 tablespoon Three-Spice Mix (page 13)

$^1/4$ teaspoon baking soda

$^3/4$ cup plus 2 tablespoons packed light or dark brown sugar

$^1/2$ cup buttermilk

2 large eggs

1 teaspoon vanilla extract

2 tablespoons granulated sugar mixed with 1 teaspoon
    Three-Spice Mix (spiced sugar)

1. Preheat the oven to 375°F. Coat an $8 \times 8 \times 2$-inch pan with nonstick cooking spray and set aside.
2. Whisk the bread mix, spice mix, and soda in a large bowl to combine. Add the brown sugar and work it in with your fingers, pressing out any lumps of sugar. Make a well in the middle of the dry ingredients. Whisk the buttermilk, eggs, and vanilla in a 1-quart measure until well blended, pour into the well, then fold in gently with a large rubber spatula to form a very stiff batter that still has a few streaks of flour showing.
3. Scoop the batter into the pan, spreading to the corners, then sprinkle the spiced sugar evenly on top. Bake in the lower third of the oven until lightly browned and a cake tester inserted in the middle of the cake comes out clean, 25 to 30 minutes.

4. Cool the cake in the pan on a wire rack to room temperature, cut into small squares, and serve.

VARIATIONS

Spicy Pecan Cake Begin as directed, but in Step 2, add 1 cup coarsely chopped pecans after you've worked in the brown sugar. Toss well to dredge, increase the amount of buttermilk to ¾ cup, then proceed as directed.

Spicy Date Cake Begin as directed, but in Step 2, add 1 cup coarsely chopped dates after you've worked in the brown sugar (I use the chopped dates now widely available). Toss well to dredge, increase the amount of buttermilk to ¾ cup, then proceed as directed.

Spicy Date-Nut Cake Begin as directed, but in Step 2, add ¾ cup each coarsely chopped dates and pecans, walnuts, or black walnuts after you've worked in the brown sugar. Toss well to dredge, increase the amount of buttermilk to 1 cup, then proceed as directed.

Spice and Raisin Cake Begin as directed, but in Step 2, add 1 cup seedless raisins after you've worked in the brown sugar. Toss well to dredge, increase the amount of buttermilk to ¾ cup, then proceed as directed.

BLACK WALNUT–BROWN SUGAR CAKE

MAKES AN 8 1/2 X 4 1/2 X 2 3/4-INCH LOAF CAKE

When I was growing up on the fringe of a southern forest, my father used to take my brother and me out to gather black walnuts. I remember their distinctive flavor—much stronger and sweeter than English walnuts. But most of all, I remember how hard their shells were and how difficult it was to extract the nut meats—one reason, no doubt, why black walnuts are seldom seen today even though these stately trees grow wild from Massachusetts to Florida and from Minnesota to Texas. Native Americans prized black walnuts and used them in cooking (they're said to be four times as nutritious as meat and, of course, contain no cholesterol). These days, however, black walnut trees are valued more as timber than as food. Luckily, there's a good source for shelled, ready-to-use nut meats—the pieces are just the right size for breads and cakes and need no chopping. For details, log onto www.sunnylandfarms.com.

> 2 cups Quick Bread Mix (page 9)
> 1/4 teaspoon baking soda
> 3/4 cup packed light brown sugar
> 1 cup coarsely chopped black walnuts or if you must use a
>   substitute, coarsely chopped pecans (see headnote)
> 3/4 cup buttermilk
> 1 extra-large egg
> 2 teaspoons vanilla extract

1. Preheat the oven to 375°F. Coat an 8½ × 4½ × 2¾-inch pan with nonstick cooking spray and set aside.
2. Whisk the bread mix and soda together in a large mixing bowl to combine. Add the brown sugar, working out any lumps with your fingers. Add the black walnuts and toss until nicely dredged. Make a well in the middle of the dry ingredients.

3. Whisk the buttermilk, egg, and vanilla in a 1-quart measure until smooth. Pour into the well in the dry ingredients, then fold in using a large rubber spatula. The batter should be lumpy with a few floury specks clearly visible.

4. Scoop the batter into the pan, spreading to the corners, and bake in the lower third of the oven until nicely browned and a cake tester inserted in the middle of the cake comes out clean, about 45 minutes.

5. Cool the cake in the upright pan on a wire rack 10 minutes, then loosen around the edge and invert on the rack. Turn right-side-up and cool to room temperature. Slice and serve as is or top, if you like, with scoops of vanilla or *dulce de leche* ice cream.

SHAKER LOAF CAKE

MAKES AN 8¹/₂ X 4¹/₂ X 2³/₄-INCH LOAF CAKE

I didn't create this novelty cake; it was developed for Presto flour more than forty years ago. The novelty of it is that you blend all ingredients by shaking them in a jar and the miracle of the recipe is that it produces a cake so good it's what a New York friend uses for his wedding cakes. The recipe here is adapted from the one in my American Century Cookbook, *a culinary nostalgia trip that begins in 1900 and proceeds right through the twentieth century.*

The best jar to use for shaking the batter is a two-quart (half-gallon) preserving jar with a lid that screws down tight, preferably a wide-mouth jar so it's easy to add the ingredients. I also use a wide-mouth canning funnel to avoid spills. The self-rising flour should be absolutely fresh so that the built-in baking powder is still plenty active. Although the recipe specifies unsifted flour, I whisk it before measuring both to lighten the flour and shatter any lumps.

> **2 large eggs**
> **³/₄ cup sugar**
> **1 teaspoon vanilla extract**
> **¹/₂ teaspoon finely grated lemon zest (optional)**
> **1 cup heavy cream**
> **1¹/₂ cups unsifted self-rising cake flour**

1. Preheat the oven to 350°F. Coat an 8¹/₂ × 4¹/₂ × 2³/₄-inch pan with nonstick oil-and-flour baking spray, then set aside.
2. Break the eggs into a 2-quart (half-gallon) preserving jar, add the sugar, screw the lid down tight, and shake hard for about 5 seconds.

3. Add the vanilla, lemon zest if using, and cream, cover tight, and shake 5 to 6 seconds until well blended. Add the flour, re-cover, and shake hard 10 times. Open the jar and using a long-handled rubber spatula, scrape the sides of the jar. Recap and shake 10 times more.

4. Pour the batter into the pan and bake in the lower third of the oven until lightly browned and a cake tester inserted in the middle of the loaf comes out clean, 45 to 50 minutes.

5. Cool the cake in the upright pan on a wire rack 15 minutes, loosen around the edge, and invert. Turn the cake right-side-up and cool to room temperature.

6. Slice about ½ inch thick and serve as is or top with freshly sliced, sweetened-to-taste peaches or strawberries and/or a scoop of vanilla, fruit, or *dulce de leche* ice cream.

DEVIL'S FOOD IN TWO SHAKES

MAKES AN 8 1/2 X 4 1/2 X 2 3/4-INCH LOAF CAKE

The Shaker Loaf Cake, which precedes, is so good and so fast I decided to see if I could make a devil's food cake the same way. Here's the result—an unusually tender-crumbed cake that's deeply chocolatey. Before preparing this cake, read the headnote for the Shaker Loaf Cake because all of the tips I offer there also apply here. This recipe calls for sweet ground chocolate with cocoa, an inspired new blend from Ghiradelli, a San Francisco company that dates back to the Gold Rush. It's available in the baking section of nearly every supermarket.

> **2 large eggs**
> **1/2 cup raw (turbinado) sugar**
> **1/3 cup sweet ground chocolate with cocoa (see headnote)**
> **1 teaspoon instant coffee crystals (preferably espresso)**
> **1 cup heavy cream**
> **1 tablespoon vanilla extract**
> **1 1/2 cups unsifted self-rising cake flour**

1. Preheat the oven to 350°F. Coat an 8½ × 4½ × 2¾-inch pan with nonstick oil-and-flour baking spray, then set aside. Or for a rich chocolate finish, coat the pan with nonstick cooking spray, then dust with unsweetened cocoa powder; tap out the excess.

2. Break the eggs into a 2-quart (half-gallon) preserving jar and add the sugar and all remaining ingredients except the flour. Screw the lid down tight and shake hard—back and forth, up and down—for 10 seconds.

3. Uncover, scrape the bottom and sides of the jar with a long-handled rubber spatula, add the flour, re-cover, and shake hard for another 10 seconds.

4. Open the jar and scrape the bottom and the sides of the jar well. Stir gently to incorporate any loose bits of flour.

5. Pour the batter into the pan and bake in the lower third of the oven until lightly browned and a cake tester inserted in the middle of the loaf comes out clean, 45 to 50 minutes.
6. Cool the cake in the upright pan on a wire rack 15 minutes, loosen around the edge, and invert. Turn the cake right-side-up and cool to room temperature.
7. Slice about ½ inch thick and serve as is or top with scoops of vanilla, chocolate, or my latest passion, *dulce de leche*, ice cream.

"ALL SHOOK UP" YELLOW CAKE
WITH CRYSTALLIZED GINGER AND PECANS

MAKES AN 8¹/₂ X 4¹/₂ X 2³/₄-INCH LOAF CAKE

Here's another jiffy loaf that's as easy as shaking everything up in a jar. As with the Shaker Loaf Cake (page 133), the heavy cream does double duty, providing both the shortening and the liquid. Read the headnote for that recipe before preparing this one because the tips I pass along there also apply here. The only time-consuming part of this recipe is chopping the crystallized ginger. Do this by hand because a food processor will churn the ginger to gum.

> **2 large eggs**
> **²/3 cup sugar**
> **2 teaspoons Three-Spice Mix (page 13)**
> **1 teaspoon vanilla extract**
> **1 cup heavy cream**
> **1¹/2 cups unsifted self-rising cake flour**
> **One 3-ounce package crystallized ginger, moderately finely
>   chopped (²/3 cup)**
> **¹/2 cup coarsely chopped pecans**

1. Preheat the oven to 350°F. Coat an 8¹/2 × 4¹/2 × 2³/4-inch pan with nonstick oil-and-flour baking spray, then set aside.
2. Break the eggs into a 2-quart (half-gallon) preserving jar and add the sugar, spice mix, vanilla, and cream. Screw the lid down tight and shake hard—back and forth, up and down—for 10 seconds.
3. Uncover, scrape the bottom and sides of the jar with a long-handled rubber spatula, add the flour, ginger, and pecans, re-cover, and shake hard for another 10 seconds.

4. Open the jar and scrape the bottom and the sides of the jar well. Stir gently to incorporate any loose bits of flour.
5. Pour the batter into the pan and bake in the lower third of the oven until lightly browned and a cake tester inserted in the middle of the loaf comes out clean, 45 to 50 minutes.
6. Cool the cake in the upright pan on a wire rack 15 minutes, loosen around the edge, and invert. Turn the cake right-side-up and cool to room temperature.
7. Slice about ½ inch thick and serve.

DENSE, DARK CHOCOLATE LOAF

MAKES AN 8 1/2 X 4 1/2 X 2 3/4-INCH LOAF CAKE

The texture of this cake is much like that of pound cake but this one goes together much faster and is also somewhat lower in calories. It doesn't need any frosting but sometimes I'll dust the top lightly with confectioners' sugar. Eat it as is or scoop some ice cream aboard each slice—chocolate, vanilla, or dulce de leche.

1 cup buttermilk
1 extra-large egg
2 teaspoons instant espresso crystals
1 tablespoon vanilla extract
2 1/2 cups Quick Cake Mix (page 12)
1/4 teaspoon baking soda
1/3 cup unsweetened cocoa powder

1. Preheat the oven to 375°F. Coat an 8½ × 4½ × 2¾-inch pan with nonstick cooking spray and set aside.
2. Combine the buttermilk, egg, espresso crystals, and vanilla in a 2-quart measure and set aside while you prepare the dry ingredients—this gives the espresso time to dissolve completely.
3. Place the cake mix and soda in a large mixing bowl, then sift in the cocoa. Using your hands, toss until the mixture is completely homogenous. Make a well in the middle.
4. Whisk the buttermilk mixture until smooth, pour into the well in the dry ingredients, then fold in gently—never beat—using a large rubber spatula until a thick, uniformly moist batter is formed. It will be stiff and lumpy, too. But that's exactly right.

5. Scoop the batter into the pan, spreading to the corners, and bake in the lower third of the oven until it smells irresistible and a cake tester inserted in the middle of the loaf comes out clean, about 45 minutes.
6. Cool the loaf in the upright pan on a wire rack 10 minutes, then loosen around the edge and invert on the rack. Turn right-side-up and cool to room temperature before slicing.

CHOCOLATE-NUT-ZUCCHINI CAKE

MAKES ONE 9 X 5 X 3-INCH LOAF CAKE

If ever a recipe begged for a food processor, it's this moist and feathery chocolate cake. If you must do everything by hand, here's how: combine the flour, sugar, and cocoa in a large bowl, then add the finely chopped nuts and toss well. Make a well in the middle of the dry ingredients. Whisk the oil, eggs, and vanilla in a two-quart measure until well blended, mix in the finely grated zucchini, then proceed as directed in Steps 5 through 7.

NOTE: *Because this makes such a full loaf, I slide a sheet of heavy-duty aluminum foil onto the oven rack before I set the pan in place—in case there's any overflow. So far there hasn't been, so this is just a precaution.*

> 1 cup pecans, walnuts, or black walnuts
> 3 cups sifted self-rising all-purpose flour
> 1^1/2 cups raw (turbinado) sugar or granulated sugar
> ^{1}/3 cup unsweetened cocoa powder
> 1^1/4 pounds tender young zucchini (about 4 small), trimmed
>   and cut into 1-inch chunks
> ^{3}/4 cup vegetable oil
> 3 large eggs
> 1 tablespoon vanilla extract

1. Preheat the oven to 375°F. Coat a 9 × 5 × 3-inch loaf pan with nonstick oil-and-flour baking spray and set aside.
2. Chop the pecans moderately fine by pulsing briskly in a food processor fitted with the metal chopping blade. Tip into a large mixing bowl.
3. Add the flour, sugar, and cocoa to the processor (no need to wash or wipe the bowl or blade) and churn for about a minute to combine. Add to the nuts, toss well, then make a well in the middle of the dry ingredients.

4. Drop the zucchini into the processor and pulse 6 to 8 times. Scrape the work bowl, then pulse 6 to 8 times more until fairly finely grated. Add the oil, eggs, and vanilla and pulse just enough to combine.
5. Pour into the well in the dry ingredients and fold in using a large rubber spatula. Do not beat. The batter will be very thick and lumpy and there should also be flecks of flour showing.
6. Scoop the batter into the pan, spreading to the corners, and bake in the lower third of the oven until richly browned and a cake tester inserted in the middle of the loaf comes out clean, about 1 hour and 10 minutes.
7. Cool the loaf in the upright pan on a wire rack 15 minutes, loosen around the edge, turn out on the rack, then cool right-side-up to room temperature before slicing.

MEXICAN CHOCOLATE CAKE

Unlike most chocolate cakes, this one is spiced with cinnamon. It needs no frosting although I do often top each slice with a scoop of vanilla ice cream or to be more Mexican, with a scoop of dulce de leche.

> **2 1/2 cups Quick Cake Mix (page 12)**
> **1 teaspoon ground cinnamon**
> **1/4 teaspoon baking soda**
> **1/4 cup unsweetened cocoa powder**
> **1 cup buttermilk**
> **2 large eggs**
> **2 teaspoons vanilla extract**

1. Preheat the oven to 375°F. Coat an 8½ × 4½ × 2¾-inch pan with nonstick cooking spray and set aside.
2. Place the cake mix, cinnamon, and soda in a large mixing bowl, then sift in the cocoa. Using your hands, toss until thoroughly mixed and make a well in the center.
3. Whisk the buttermilk, eggs, and vanilla in a 2-quart measure until smooth. Pour into the well in the dry ingredients and fold in with a large rubber spatula. It's easiest if you draw the dry ingredients into combined liquids, turning the bowl as you go, and folding gently—never beating—until a thick, uniformly moist batter is formed. It will be lumpy and that's entirely correct.
4. Scoop the batter into the pan, spread to the corners, and bake in the lower third of the oven until a cake tester inserted in the middle of the loaf comes out clean, 45 minutes.
5. Cool the loaf in the upright pan on a wire rack 10 minutes, then loosen around the edge and invert on the rack. Turn right-side-up and cool to room temperature before slicing.

KIDS'LL LOVE IT CHOCOLATE CHIP CAKE

MAKES AN 8 X 8 X 2-INCH LOAF CAKE

America's favorite cookie turned into a cake so quick and easy the kids will want to help. One note of caution: because of its richness, this cake tends to overbrown if baked in a dark pan, so use a silvery one that reflects the heat. Also, bake the cake on the middle oven shelf.

$2^1/2$ cups Quick Bread Mix (page 9)
$3/4$ raw (turbinado) sugar
$1/4$ teaspoon baking soda
$3/4$ cup coarsely chopped pecans
$3/4$ cup chocolate chips
$1/2$ cup milk
2 large eggs
$1^1/2$ teaspoons vanilla extract

1. Preheat the oven to 375°F. Coat an $8 \times 8 \times 2$-inch pan with nonstick oil-and-flour baking spray and aside.
2. Whisk the bread mix, sugar, and soda in a large mixing bowl to combine. Add the pecans and chocolate chips and toss well. Make a well in the middle of the dry ingredients.
3. Whisk the milk, eggs, and vanilla in a 1-quart measure until well blended. Pour into the well in the dry ingredients, then fold in using a large rubber spatula to form a very stiff dough.
4. Scoop the dough into the pan, pushing to the corners, and bake on the middle oven shelf until richly browned and a cake tester inserted in the middle of the cake comes out clean, 40 to 45 minutes.
5. Cool the cake in the upright pan on a wire rack to room temperature, cut into small squares, and serve.

CHOCOLATE–PEANUT BUTTER CRUMB CAKE

MAKES AN 8 X 8 X 2-INCH LOAF CAKE

Chocolate and peanuts are one of those made-in-heaven marriages and this fudgy cake with the crunchy peanut topping proves the point. To prevent overbrowning, I bake the cake in a silvery pan (dark ones absorb and hold heat) on the middle oven shelf at a temperature slightly lower than that used for most of my other quick cakes.

CAKE

2^1/2 cups Quick Cake Mix (page 12)

^{1}/3 cup unsweetened cocoa powder (to get rid of lumps, I sift
   it directly into the mixing bowl)

^{1}/4 teaspoon baking soda

^{3}/4 cup chocolate chips

^{3}/4 cup peanut butter chips

^{3}/4 cup milk

2 large eggs

2 teaspoons vanilla extract

TOPPING

^{1}/2 cup Quick Cake Mix

^{1}/2 cup moderately finely chopped, lightly salted cocktail
   peanuts

1. Preheat the oven to 350°F. Coat an 8 × 8 × 2-inch pan with nonstick oil-and-flour baking spray and aside.
2. CAKE: Whisk the cake mix, cocoa, and soda together in a large mixing bowl to combine. Add the chocolate and peanut butter chips and toss until nicely dredged. Make a well in the middle of the dry ingredients.

3. Whisk the milk, eggs, and vanilla in a 1-quart measure until well blended. Pour into the well in the dry ingredients, then fold in using a large rubber spatula to form a very stiff batter. Scoop into the pan, spreading to the corners.

4. TOPPING: Quickly combine the topping ingredients and scatter evenly over the cake. Slide onto the middle oven shelf and bake until richly browned and a cake tester inserted in the middle of the cake comes out clean, 50 to 55 minutes.

5. Cool the cake in the upright pan on a wire rack to room temperature, cut into small squares, and serve.

CHOCOLATE MARBLE CAKE

MAKES AN 8 X 8 X 2-INCH LOAF CAKE

When I was a little girl, the cake I most loved to make was marble cake. I did it the old-fashioned way, stirring up a yellow cake batter, then blending half of it with a little melted chocolate. The part I liked best was swirling alternate scoops of dark and light batter in the pan until they resembled marble. This short-cut version is a good snacking cake—great with a cup of coffee, a cup of tea, or a glass of milk.

NOTE: *Choose a dry, sunny day for making this cake. In wet or humid weather, the chocolate absorbs atmospheric moisture and becomes sticky.*

> **2 1/2 cups Quick Cake Mix (page 12)**
> **1/2 cup milk**
> **2 large eggs**
> **1 tablespoon vanilla extract**
> **1/2 cup sweet ground chocolate with cocoa blended with**
> > **1/4 cup milk (see headnote for Devil's Food in Two**
> > **Shakes, page 135)**

1. Preheat the oven to 350°F. Coat an 8 × 8 × 2-inch pan with nonstick cooking spray and set aside.
2. Place the cake mix in a large bowl and make a well in the middle. Whisk the milk, eggs, and vanilla in a 1-quart measure until well blended, pour into the well, then fold in gently but completely using a large rubber spatula.
3. Scoop the batter into the pan, spreading to the corners. Using a tablespoon, drop the chocolate mixture on the batter making three rows of three (think tick-tack-

toe). Using the same spoon, scoop down through each chocolate puddle, bringing the yellow batter up on top. Continue until the cake is well marbled, but work gently, never ever beating.

4. Bake the cake in the lower third of the oven until lightly browned and a cake tester inserted in the middle comes out clean, 35 to 40 minutes.

5. Cool the cake in the pan on a wire rack to room temperature, cut into squares, and serve.

GOLDEN GINGERBREAD WITH DRIED BLUEBERRIES

MAKES A 9 X 9 X 2-INCH LOAF

I used to make a gingerbread somewhat like this but it called for fresh blueberries, which had to be washed, stemmed, and patted very dry—a nuisance. Now that dried blueberries are widely available, I decided to give them a try and they're perfect here. I also use my Quick Cake Mix to jump-start this recipe and it's in the oven in less than ten minutes. You'll find this gingerbread picnic-perfect—it can be made ahead of time and its pan becomes the carrier.

3 cups Quick Cake Mix (page 12)
1 teaspoon Three-Spice Mix (page 13)
1 teaspoon ground ginger
1/4 teaspoon baking soda
One 3-ounce package dried blueberries (3/4 cup)
2/3 cup buttermilk
2 tablespoons molasses (not too dark)
2 large eggs
2 tablespoons sugar blended with 1/2 teaspoon Three-Spice
    Mix (spiced sugar)

1. Preheat the oven to 375°F. Coat a 9 × 9 × 2-inch pan with nonstick oil-and-flour baking spray, then set aside.
2. Whisk the cake and spice mixes, the ginger, and soda together in a large bowl to combine. Add the berries and toss well. Make a well in the middle of the dry ingredients.
3. Whisk the buttermilk, molasses, and eggs in a 1-quart measure until smooth. Pour into the well in the dry ingredients, then fold in using a large rubber spatula. The batter should be lumpy with a few floury specks clearly visible.

4. Scoop the batter into the pan, spreading to the corners, and sprinkle the spiced sugar evenly on top. Bake in the lower third of the oven until lightly browned and a cake tester inserted in the middle of the gingerbread comes out clean, 25 to 30 minutes.

5. Cool the gingerbread in the upright pan on a wire rack to room temperature, cut into large squares, and serve.

APPLE UPSIDE-DOWN GINGERBREAD

MAKES A 10-INCH ROUND LOAF

If I had to peel, core, and slice a pound and a half of apples, then bake them with sugar and cinnamon, this gingerbread would hardly be quick. So I use frozen, cinnamony baked apples instead—a popular national brand sold at every supermarket. In addition, my Quick Cake Mix jump-starts the gingerbread. To grate fresh ginger in jig time, I use a microplane, which is simply a culinary version of a carpenter's rasp. This amazing new gadget grates things in seconds and the shreds don't stick to it.

Two solidly frozen 12-ounce packages "Harvest Apples"
  (Jonathans baked with cinnamon)
3 cups Quick Cake Mix (page 12)
1 tablespoon Three-Spice Mix (page 13)
1/2 teaspoon baking soda
1 cup milk
1/2 cup light molasses
1/3 cup finely grated fresh ginger (see headnote)
1 teaspoon grated lemon zest
2 large eggs

1. Coat a well-seasoned 10-inch cast-iron skillet generously with nonstick cooking spray, unwrap the frozen apples, and place in the skillet. Set the skillet on a rack in the lower third of the oven and preheat the oven to 375°F.
2. Whisk the cake mix, spice mix, and soda in a large bowl to combine, then make a well in the middle of the dry ingredients.

3. Whisk the milk, molasses, ginger, lemon zest, and eggs in a 2-quart measure until well blended. Pour into the well in the dry ingredients and gently fold in—don't beat—using a large rubber spatula until uniformly moist. The batter will be stiff and lumpy.

4. Remove the hot skillet from the oven, spread the apples evenly over the bottom, and scoop the batter on top, smoothing to the edge all round. Bake in the lower third of the oven until lightly browned and a cake tester inserted in the middle of the gingerbread comes out clean, 45 to 50 minutes.

5. Cool the gingerbread in the upright skillet on a wire rack 10 minutes, then loosen around the edge, and invert on a large round platter. Inevitably, some of the apples will stick to the bottom of the skillet—no problem. Simply scoop them up and set them back in place. No one will know.

6. Cool the gingerbread 10 to 15 minutes more, cut into wedges, and serve warm. Drift each portion with a little softly whipped cream, if you like, or top with a scoop of vanilla ice cream.

SCOTTISH GINGER CAKE

MAKES AN 8 X 8 X 2-INCH LOAF CAKE

This intensely gingery gingerbread contains three kinds of ginger—fresh, preserved, and ground. It also contains beer as the liquid ingredient—a wonderful complement to the ginger. I chop the fresh ginger in a food processor—several longish pulses is all it takes. The variation is an old, old, old family recipe.

2¹/2 cups Quick Cake Mix (page 12)

1 teaspoon Three-Spice Mix (page 13)

1 teaspoon ground ginger

¹/4 teaspoon baking soda

¹/2 cup stale beer

¹/2 cup finely chopped fresh ginger (for this amount you'll
   need 3¹/2 ounces ginger)

2 tablespoons molasses (not too dark)

2 tablespoons ginger preserves

2 large eggs

1. Preheat the oven to 375°F. Coat an 8 × 8 × 2-inch pan with nonstick oil-and-flour baking spray and set aside.
2. Whisk the cake and spice mixes, the ground ginger, and soda in a large bowl until well combined. Make a well in the middle of the dry ingredients.
3. Whisk the beer, chopped ginger, molasses, preserves, and eggs in a 1-quart measure until well blended, pour into the well in the dry ingredients, and fold in using a large rubber spatula. The batter should be lumpy and about the texture of biscuit dough. It's good if a few floury streaks show.

4. Scoop the batter into the pan, pushing to the corners, and bake in the lower third of the oven until the gingerbread is richly browned and a cake tester stuck in the middle comes out clean, 30 to 35 minutes.

5. Cool the gingerbread in the upright pan on a wire rack to room temperature, cut into squares, and serve.

VARIATION

Graham Clan Gingerbread with Raisins In Step 2, combine ½ teaspoon freshly ground black pepper with the dry ingredients, then before folding in the combined liquids, add ¼ cup each golden raisins and seedless brown raisins or dried currants and toss until nicely dredged. Otherwise, proceed as directed.

OLD YORKSHIRE SEED CAKE

MAKES AN 8 X 8 X 2-INCH LOAF CAKE

Nearly every English county has its own seed cake, but this one from Brontë country is one of the best. I like to imagine Jane Eyre (or Heathcliff and Cathy) taking it with tea after a morning on the moors.

2^1/2 cups Quick Cake Mix (page 12)

^{1}/4 cup unsifted all-purpose flour

2 teaspoons Three-Spice Mix (page 13)

2 teaspoons caraway seeds

^{1}/2 cup coarsely chopped sliced or slivered almonds or
   coarsely chopped walnuts

^{1}/2 cup diced mixed candied fruits

^{1}/2 cup milk

2 large eggs

1. Preheat the oven to 375°F. Coat an 8 × 8 × 2-inch loaf pan with nonstick oil-and-flour baking spray and set aside.

2. Whisk the cake mix, flour, spice mix, and caraway seeds in a large bowl until well combined. Add the almonds and candied fruits and toss until nicely dredged. Make a well in the middle of the dry ingredients.

3. Whisk the milk and eggs in a 1-quart measure until well blended, pour into the well in the dry ingredients, and fold in using a large rubber spatula. The dough should be lumpy—about the texture of biscuit dough with a few floury streaks showing.

4. Scoop the dough into the pan, pushing to the corners, and bake in the lower third of the oven until the cake is richly browned and a cake tester stuck in the middle comes out clean, 35 to 40 minutes.

5. Cool the cake in the pan on a wire rack to room temperature, cut into small squares, and serve.

FAST FRUITCAKE

MAKES AN 8 1/2 X 4 1/2 X 2 3/4-INCH LOAF CAKE

I think this one-hour fruitcake beats the old-fashioned kind nine ways to Sunday, but then I've never liked leaden Christmas cakes. This loaf is delicious as is, but traditionalists may want to wrap it in rum- or bourbon-soaked cheesecloth and let it "season" for several days.

2 1/2 cups Quick Cake Mix (page 12)
2 teaspoons Five-Spice Mix (page 14)
1 cup coarsely chopped pecans
One 7-ounce package dried fruit bits
1/2 cup diced dates (I buy them already diced)
1 cup milk
1/4 cup ginger preserves
2 large eggs
1 teaspoon vanilla extract

1. Preheat the oven to 375°F. Coat an 8½ × 4½ × 2¾-inch pan with nonstick oil-and-flour baking spray and set aside.

2. Place the cake mix and spice mix in a large bowl and whisk to combine. Add the pecans, fruit bits, and dates and toss well. Make a well in the middle of the dry ingredients.

3. Whisk the milk, ginger preserves, eggs, and vanilla in a 2-quart measure until well blended. Pour into the well in the dry ingredients, then fold in using a large rubber spatula. The batter will be thick and lumpy—exactly as it should be.

4. Scoop the batter into the pan, spreading to the corners, and bake in the lower third of the oven until nicely browned and a cake tester inserted in the middle of the loaf comes out clean, 45 to 50 minutes.

5. Cool the loaf in the upright pan on a wire rack 10 minutes, then loosen around the edge and invert on the rack. Turn right-side-up and cool to room temperature before slicing.

TROPICAL FRUITCAKE

Supermarkets now carry such an array of dried tropical fruits that I thought it would be fun to develop a quick fruitcake that put them to good use. I think this one does.

2¹/2 cups Quick Cake Mix (page 12)

1 teaspoon Five-Spice Mix (page 14)

¹/4 teaspoon baking soda

¹/3 cup moderately finely diced dried mango or papaya

¹/3 cup moderately finely diced dried pineapple

¹/3 cup plus 2 tablespoons sweetened flaked coconut

¹/2 cup milk

2 tablespoons orange marmalade

2 large eggs

1. Preheat the oven to 375°F. Coat an 8½ × 4½ × 2¾-inch loaf pan with nonstick oil-and-flour baking spray and set aside.

2. Whisk the cake and spice mixes and soda in a large bowl until well combined. Add the mango, pineapple, and the ⅓ cup of coconut and toss until nicely dredged. Make a well in the middle of the dry ingredients.

3. Whisk the milk, marmalade, and eggs in a 1-quart measure until well blended, pour into the well in the dry ingredients, and fold in using a large rubber spatula to form a dough about the texture of biscuit dough. It's good if there are a few floury streaks.

4. Scoop the dough into the pan, pushing to the corners. Sprinkle with the remaining 2 tablespoons coconut and bake in the lower third of the oven for 25 minutes. Cover loosely with foil (to keep the coconut from overbrowning) and continue baking until a cake tester stuck in the middle of the cake comes out clean, 20 to 25 minutes longer.

5. Cool the cake in the upright pan on a wire rack 15 minutes, loosen around the edge, turn out on the rack, then cool right-side-up to room temperature before slicing.

SPICY BROWN SUGAR RAISIN CAKE

MAKES A 10-INCH TUBE CAKE

According to my good friend and colleague Joanne Lamb Hayes, women were baking an eggless cake much like this one back during the Civil War. She found a handwritten recipe for this "War Cake" in an early 1900s booklet. And because it was so popular during World War II, she included the recipe for it in her fascinating cookbook, Grandma's Wartime Kitchen: World War II and the Way We Cooked *(St. Martin's Press, 2000). The recipe here is my speeded-up variation.*

> 1 pound seedless raisins
> 2 cups packed light brown sugar
> 2 cups water
> 1/4 cup packed vegetable shortening or lard
> 1 tablespoon Three-Spice Mix (page 13)
> 1/2 teaspoon salt
> 3 cups unsifted all-purpose flour combined with 2 teaspoons
>   baking soda

1. Preheat the oven to 350°F. Coat a 10-inch tube pan with nonstick oil-and-flour baking spray and set aside.
2. Bring the raisins, brown sugar, water, shortening, spice mix, and salt to a boil in a large heavy saucepan over moderate heat, then cook for 5 minutes, stirring now and then. Cool the raisin mixture to room temperature—setting the pan in an ice bath will speed things along but you should stir the mixture frequently.
3. Fold the flour-soda mixture into the cooled raisin mixture, then scoop the batter into the tube pan, spreading to the edge.

4. Bake the cake in the lower third of the oven until richly browned and a cake tester inserted midway between the central tube and the side of the pan comes out clean, 45 to 50 minutes.
5. Cool the cake in the upright pan on a wire rack 10 minutes. Loosen around the edge and around the central tube using a thin-blade metal spatula, then invert the cake on a wire rack and cool to room temperature before cutting.

MOLASSES CASSEROLE CAKE

MAKES 6 TO 8 SERVINGS

Here's an easy version of an Old South cake that bakes in a soufflé dish. Unmolded, the cake has the texture of plum pudding, and like it, is good topped with whipped cream.

> 2 cups Quick Bread Mix (page 9)
> 2 teaspoons Five-Spice Mix (page 14)
> 1/4 teaspoon baking soda
> 1/2 cup packed light brown sugar
> 3/4 cup golden seedless raisins
> 1/2 cup molasses (not too dark)
> 1/2 cup water
> 2 large eggs
> 2 tablespoons finely grated fresh ginger

1. Preheat the oven to 350°F. Coat a 2-quart soufflé dish with nonstick cooking spray and set aside.
2. Place the bread mix, spice mix, and soda in a large bowl and whisk well to combine. Add the brown sugar, working in with your hands, then add the raisins and toss well. Make a well in the middle of the dry ingredients.
3. Whisk the molasses, water, eggs, and grated ginger together in a 1-quart measure until well blended. Pour into the well in the dry ingredients, then fold in using a large rubber spatula. The batter will be thick and lumpy.

4. Scoop into the soufflé dish, spreading to the edge, and bake in the lower third of the oven until deeply brown and a cake tester inserted in the middle of the cake comes out clean, about 30 minutes.

5. Cool the cake in the upright soufflé dish on a wire rack 10 minutes, then loosen around the edge and invert on a round platter.

6. Cool to room temperature, cut into wedges, and serve—with or without whipped cream.

ORANGE–POPPY SEED CAKE

MAKES AN 8 1/2 X 4 1/2 X 2 3/4-INCH LOAF

Make sure the poppy seeds you use are absolutely fresh because if they are rancid, they will spread their acrid taste throughout the cake.

CAKE

2 1/2 cups Quick Cake Mix (page 12)

1/4 cup unsifted all-purpose flour

2 tablespoons poppy seeds

1/4 teaspoon baking soda

3/4 cup buttermilk

1 extra-large egg

2 tablespoons finely grated orange zest

1 teaspoon orange extract

OPTIONAL GLAZE

1/2 cup unsifted confectioners' (10X) sugar whisked until smooth with 1 tablespoon fresh orange juice

1. Preheat the oven to 375°F. Coat an 8½ × 4½ × 2¾-inch loaf pan with nonstick cooking spray and set aside.
2. Whisk the cake mix, flour, poppy seeds, and soda in a large bowl to combine, then make a well in the middle of the dry ingredients.
3. Whisk the buttermilk, egg, orange zest, and orange extract in a 2-quart measure until well blended. Pour into the well in the dry ingredients and gently fold in until uniformly moist—don't beat—using a large rubber spatula. The batter should be stiff and lumpy.

4. Scoop the batter into the pan, spreading to the corners, and bake in the lower third of the oven until lightly browned and a cake tester inserted in the middle of the loaf comes out clean, about 45 minutes.

5. Cool the loaf in the upright pan on a wire rack 10 minutes, loosen around the edge, turn out on the rack, then cool right-side-up to room temperature.

6. Glaze the loaf, if you like—just drizzle it over the top—and let stand 15 to 20 minutes before slicing.

VARIATIONS

Lemon–Poppy Seed Loaf Prepare as directed substituting the finely grated zest of 1 large lemon for the orange zest and omitting the orange extract. If you glaze the loaf, prepare the glaze as directed substituting 1 tablespoon fresh lemon juice for orange juice.

Grapefruit–Poppy Seed Loaf Prepare as directed substituting 2 tablespoons finely grated grapefruit zest for orange zest and omitting the orange extract. If you glaze the loaf, use 1 tablespoon fresh grapefruit juice in the glaze instead of orange juice.

HONEY-LEMON POLENTA CAKE

MAKES AN 8 1/2 X 4 1/2 X 2 3/4-INCH LOAF CAKE

One of my favorite places to eat in New York is Periyali, a high-end Greek restaurant in the Chelsea district. Because I love Periyali's polenta cake, I wanted to work up an easy version using my Quick Cake Mix. It took me half a dozen tries to produce the tall, dense loaf I wanted. At first, my loaves kept sinking in the middle—a problem with honey cakes as well as with those containing too much sugar. To solve the problem, I substituted my Quick Bread Mix for my cake mix, which allowed me to control the amount of sugar. Polenta, if you don't know it, is cornmeal ground a little finer than table salt— the way Italians like it. Once available mainly in Italian groceries, polenta is now a staple in nearly every supermarket. Look for it in the pasta section and choose the quick-cooking variety. I like polenta cake straight up even though it has the texture of cornbread. If you prefer, top each portion with sliced, sweetened-to-taste fresh strawberries or peaches and/or a scoop of vanilla ice cream.

CAKE

2 cups Quick Bread Mix (page 9)

1 cup quick-cooking polenta

1/2 cup sugar

1/2 teaspoon baking soda

1 cup buttermilk

1/4 cup light honey

Finely grated zest of 1 large lemon

1 extra-large egg

SYRUP

2 tablespoons light honey

2 tablespoons hot water

1 tablespoon fresh lemon juice

1. Preheat the oven to 375°F. Coat an 8½ × 4½ × 2¾-inch pan with nonstick spray and set aside.

2. CAKE: Place the bread mix, polenta, sugar, and soda in a large mixing bowl, then using your hands, toss until the mixture is completely homogenous. Make a well in the middle.

3. Whisk the buttermilk, honey, lemon zest, and egg in a 2-quart measure until smooth. Pour into the well in the dry ingredients, then fold in using a large rubber spatula. It's easiest if you draw the dry ingredients into the puddle of combined liquids, turning the bowl as you go, and folding gently—never beating—until a thick, uniformly moist batter is formed. It will be lumpy and that's as it should be.

4. Scoop the batter into the pan, spreading to the corners, and bake in the lower third of the oven until nicely browned and a cake tester inserted in the middle of the loaf comes out clean, about 45 minutes.

5. Cool the loaf in the upright pan on a wire rack 15 minutes, then loosen around the edge and invert on the rack. Turn right-side-up and cool to room temperature.

6. Quickly combine the syrup ingredients, then brush over the top and sides of the cake. Let stand 15 minutes before cutting.

ANY-TIME-OF-YEAR SUMMER PUDDING

MAKES 8 SERVINGS

With frozen berries available all year-round, there's every reason to make this pudding-loaf in fall, winter, and spring as well as in summer. Old-fashioned English summer puddings are most often made with stale bread, but the firm-textured white loaf I always used now just turns gluey. Perhaps the baker has changed the recipe. Whatever the reason, I use frozen pound cake. This pudding is the perfect party make-ahead because it must chill overnight.

Two 16-ounce bags frozen unsweetened mixed berries, thawed, with their liquid

One 12-ounce bag frozen unsweetened raspberries, thawed, with their liquid

1/4 cup Grand Marnier or other orange liqueur or 1 teaspoon orange extract

1 tablespoon sugar

Two 10.75-ounce frozen pound cakes, thawed

1. Combine all of the berries, the Grand Marnier, and sugar in a large bowl and let stand while you line a smaller bowl with cake.

2. Cut each pound cake lengthwise into 10 slices 1/4 inch thick. Lay 3 brown-edge slices side by side on a cutting board and invert a deep 2-quart metal bowl measuring about 7 inches across the top directly on top of them. Cut around the bowl so that you have a circle of slices; set these aside along with the scraps. Line the bowl with plastic wrap, letting the ends overhang 5 or 6 inches all around.

3. Halve one cake slice crosswise, then place the two pieces side by side on the cutting board with edges abutting. Using a 3-inch round cookie cutter or a jar lid, cut out a circle 3 inches in diameter. Brush with some of the berry liquid and place brushed-side-down in the bottom of the plastic-lined bowl.

4. Beginning at one end and trimming from each side, taper each of 14 slices into an elongated wedge that's just ¾ inch wide at the small end. Brush each cake wedge with berry liquid, then line the bowl by standing the wedges points down and brushed sides against the bowl. Press some of the scraps into any gaps between cake wedges and trim off any excess at top. Save all trimmings.

5. Cut the remaining cake and all scraps into ½-inch cubes and stir into the mixed berries. Spoon all into the cake-lined mold and top with the cut-to-fit 7-inch circle of slices. Smooth the plastic wrap overhang over the cake, covering it completely. Place a saucer on top and weight with something heavy. Refrigerate overnight.

6. When ready to serve, remove the weights and saucer, unwrap the top of the cake, and pull on the edges of the plastic wrap to loosen. Invert the summer pudding on a serving plate and remove the plastic wrap.

7. To serve, cut into wedges and accompany, if you like, with softly whipped cream.

TWO-TONE CHOCOLATE AND VANILLA RICE PUDDING LOAF

MAKES 12 SERVINGS

If you're like me, you always cook more rice than you need or have gobs of it left over from Chinese take-out. Here's a delicious way to use the excess.

NOTE: *This loaf must chill overnight so plan accordingly.*

One 6-ounce package chocolate-filled lady-finger-shaped
    butter cookies (I use "Milanos")
2¹/2 cups milk
1/2 cup sugar blended with 1/4 cup cornstarch
3 cups leftover cooked rice, preferably short- or medium-
    grain
2 teaspoons vanilla extract
1/3 cup semisweet chocolate chips
1 teaspoon unsweetened cocoa powder

1. Line a $9 \times 5 \times 3$-inch loaf pan with baking parchment, letting it overhang the sides; set aside. Trim ½ inch off one end of 12 cookies. Pop the trimmings into a plastic bag along with the remaining cookies and bang with a rolling pin until coarsely crushed.

2. Bring 2 cups of the milk to a boil in a large saucepan over moderate heat. Meanwhile, blend the remaining milk with the sugar–cornstarch mixture. Whisk into the boiling milk and cook, stirring, just until it returns to a boil. Off heat, mix in the rice and vanilla. Measure out 1¼ cups of the rice mixture, add the chocolate chips, and stir until melted.

3. Spread a thin layer of vanilla rice pudding in the bottom of the pan, then stand 6 cookies, trimmed ends down, along each long side of the pan. Alternately drop spoonfuls of chocolate and vanilla rice pudding into the pan. When half of each has been used, sprinkle in the crushed cookies, then continue filling the pan as before. Smooth the top.

4. Cool 30 minutes, tightly wrap the pan in foil or plastic food wrap, and refrigerate overnight.

5. To serve, gently lift the pudding loaf onto a platter using the parchment overhang as handles. Slide a thin-blade metal spatula underneath the loaf, then gently ease out the parchment.

6. Sift the cocoa over the top of the loaf, slice it crosswise, cutting between the cookies, then halve it lengthwise, and serve.

FROZEN TUTTI-FRUTTI PARTY LOAF

MAKES 10 TO 12 SERVINGS

Southerners are famous for their sweet tooth, and when I was growing up below the Mason-Dixon, everyone was into frozen fruit salads, "salad" being a euphemism for dessert. Most were loaded with mayo (the reason they were called salads?), marshmallows, and maraschinos. Oh yes, and plenty of whipped cream. Frozen fruit salads are still immensely popular as a look at any community fund-raising cookbook will prove. In developing this party dessert, I put a new spin on the old frozen fruit salad. Gone are the mayo, marshmallows, and maraschinos, and in their place, a pound of frozen, unsweetened mixed berries. I also substituted sour cream for whipped because it contains less fat and fewer calories.

For this recipe, I like the slivered almonds well toasted—eight to ten minutes in a 350°F oven is about right if you spread them on a small baking sheet and stir well at halftime, but watch carefully. Use reduced-fat sour cream and sweetened condensed milk, if you like. I prefer regular because they make a smoother, more flavorful loaf. This dessert should freeze overnight, so prepare it the day before you plan to serve. I often make it weeks ahead, wrap it snugly in foil, and store in the freezer.

One 14-ounce can sweetened condensed milk

1 cup sour cream (measure firmly packed)

1 tablespoon vanilla or rum extract

One 1-pound, 4-ounce can crushed pineapple, drained well
   and pressed dry

1 cup chopped dates (I buy them already chopped, to save
   time)

1 cup nicely toasted slivered almonds (see headnote)

One 1-pound package solidly frozen unsweetened mixed
   berries (blueberries, blackberries, raspberries,
   strawberries)

1. Lightly spritz a 10 × 5 × 3-inch loaf pan with nonstick cooking spray and set aside.

2. Whisk the sweetened condensed milk, sour cream, and vanilla until smooth in a large bowl. Add the pineapple, dates, and almonds and mix well. Fold in the solidly frozen berries. Scoop all into the pan and freeze until firm—preferably overnight.

3. To unmold, dip the pan briefly in hot water, loosen the loaf around the edge with a thin-blade metal spatula, and invert on a double thickness of heavy-duty aluminum foil. Smooth the top and sides of the loaf with the spatula, then set in the freezer—without wrapping—for 30 minutes. Wrap the loaf in the foil and store in the freezer until about 15 minutes before serving. This loaf is prettier sliced than whole and cuts more neatly when solidly frozen.

4. Using a sharp, heavy serrated knife and a see-saw motion, cut the frozen loaf into slices ¾ to 1 inch thick. Transfer the slices to colorful dessert plates and let stand (temper) 10 to 15 minutes before serving.

FROZEN FRANGELICO TORTE

MAKES 12 SERVINGS

Remember those thin, round chocolate wafers that we used to make zebra cakes and crumb pie crusts? I wanted them for this recipe but couldn't find them, so I substituted other plain chocolate cookies—no frosting, no filling, and they worked just fine.

TIP: *The fastest ways to reduce cookies to crumbs are to slip them into a plastic bag and bang with a rolling pin, or even easier, buzz in a food processor fitted with the metal chopping blade.*

I grind the hazelnuts by machine (six to eight long pulses), then mix the filling there, too: I place the sour cream, Frangelico, vanilla, and cream cheese in the work bowl in that order, add the chocolate mixture while it's still hot, and churn until smooth.

NOTE: *This torte is both sweet and tangy—a combination I find refreshing. For less tartness, omit the cream cheese, whip one cup heavy cream softly, and fold in at the end.*

2 cups fine chocolate cookie crumbs

1 cup lightly toasted hazelnuts (page 16), finely ground

6 tablespoons (³/4 stick) butter, melted

One 14-ounce can sweetened condensed milk

1 cup semisweet chocolate chips (about one 6-ounce
    package)

One 8-ounce package light cream cheese (Neufchâtel),
    at room temperature

2 cups sour cream (one 16-ounce container)

¹/3 cup Frangelico or other hazelnut liqueur

1 teaspoon vanilla extract

1. Combine the cookie crumbs, ground hazelnuts, and melted butter in a small bowl. Scoop out ½ cup of the mixture—this will be the topping. Lightly spritz an 8- or 9-inch springform pan with nonstick cooking spray, then pat half of the remaining crumb mixture firmly over the bottom. Set aside.

2. Place the milk and chocolate chips in a heavy medium saucepan, set over low heat, and cook, stirring occasionally, until the chocolate melts, 8 to 10 minutes. Add the cream cheese, breaking it into small chunks, and stir until smooth. Remove from the heat and blend in the sour cream, Frangelico, and vanilla.

3. Pour half of the chocolate mixture into the springform pan, smoothing to the edges, sprinkle with the other half of the cookie crumb mixture, distributing evenly. Pour in the remaining filling, then scatter on the reserved topping. Cover with aluminum foil and freeze several hours or overnight until firm.

4. To serve, dip a thin-blade metal spatula in hot water and loosen the torte around the edge. Remove the springform pan sides. I usually leave the torte on the pan bottom and set it on a bright round platter. If you work carefully, however, you can free the torte from the pan bottom using a broad metal spatula and dipping as needed in hot water.

VARIATION

Frozen Amaretto Torte Prepare as directed, substituting 1 cup lightly toasted slivered almonds for the hazelnuts and Amaretto for Frangelico. I also usually omit the cream cheese and after blending in the sour cream, liqueur, and vanilla, fold in 1 cup heavy cream that has been softly whipped. Finally, I will sometimes use milk chocolate chips instead of semisweet.

ZIP-QUICK TORTONI

MAKES 12 SERVINGS

A terrific party make-ahead that can be kept in the freezer for weeks. The only time-consuming part is crushing the cookies—two to three minutes if you slip them into a plastic bag and pound with a rolling pin, about thirty seconds of pulsing in a food processor. The only cookies to use are the crunchy, intensely almond Amaretti di Saronno imported from Italy. Most specialty food shops sell them. Properly crushed, the cookie crumbs should be a little coarser than kosher salt.

One 14-ounce can sweetened condensed milk
$1/2$ cup half-and-half
$1/4$ cup Amaretto liqueur or $1/2$ teaspoon almond extract
1 teaspoon vanilla extract
1 cup heavy cream, softly whipped
Eight $1^1/2$-inch Amaretti di Saronno cookies, moderately
    coarsely crushed

1. Line 12 muffin-pan cups with crinkly foil or paper liners and set aside. (I use two 6-muffin pans instead of a single 12-muffin pan because it's easier to find freezer room for them.)
2. Whisk the condensed milk, half-and-half, Amaretto, and vanilla together in a large bowl until smooth. Add the whipped cream and using the whisk, fold in until absolutely smooth. Ladle into the muffin pans, then lightly strew each tortoni with cookie crumbs.
3. Set in the freezer and freeze several hours or until firm. Once the tortoni are hard, you can remove them from the muffin pans, pop into a plastic zipper bag, and store in the freezer.
4. Serve the tortoni in the foil or paper liners or, if you prefer, peel these off—but you'll have to work fast because once the tortoni begin to soften, the liners don't come off neatly.

FROZEN KEY LIME MOUSSES

MAKES 12 SERVINGS

If you can buy fresh Key limes, by all means use them here. Otherwise, settle for bottled Key lime juice—many boutique groceries carry it. You may want to tint the mousse mixture a pale lime green—just one drop of green food coloring and another of yellow. I prefer the filling's natural ivory color, and garnish each mousse with a twist of lime and dab of whipped cream.

One 14-ounce can sweetened condensed milk
$1/2$ cup fresh or bottled Key lime juice
Finely grated zest of $1/2$ green Persian lime (do not use Key lime)
$1^1/2$ cups heavy cream, softly whipped
1 drop each green and yellow food coloring (optional)

OPTIONAL GARNISHES
$1/2$ cup heavy cream, softly whipped
12 thin slices green Persian lime, each cut along one radius from rind to center, then twisted into an S-shape

1. Line two 6-cup muffin pans with crinkly foil or paper liners and set aside.
2. Whisk the condensed milk, Key lime juice, and zest together in a large bowl to combine. Add the whipped cream and whisk until smooth. To tint pale lime, mix in the green and yellow food colorings. Ladle the mixture into the muffin pans, and freeze several hours or until firm. When the mousses are solidly frozen, you can remove them from the pans, pop into a plastic zipper bag, and store in the freezer.
3. To serve, quickly peel the paper wrappers from the mousses, then garnish each, if you like, by drifting with whipped cream and adding a twist of lime.

LITTLE CUPS OF MOCHA GELATO

MAKES 12 SERVINGS

True Sicilian gelato (ice cream) is custard-based. My short-cut version requires no egg and no cooking, yet freezes to egg-custard smoothness. It's incredibly easy and even more so if you use a food processor fitted with the metal chopping blade: whiz the first six ingredients for fifteen to twenty seconds until smooth, then scrape all into a large bowl. Add the heavy cream to the machine (no need to wash or rinse work bowl or blade), churn ten to fifteen seconds until softly whipped, then fold in as directed in Step 2. Proceed according to the recipe.

> One 14-ounce can sweetened condensed milk
> One 5-ounce can fat-free evaporated milk
> 1/4 cup unsweetened cocoa powder
> 1/4 cup Tia Maria, Kahlúa, or other coffee or chocolate
>   liqueur
> 2 tablespoons instant espresso crystals
> 1 teaspoon vanilla extract
> 1 cup heavy cream, softly whipped

OPTIONAL GARNISHES
> 1/2 cup heavy cream, softly whipped
> One 1-ounce square semisweet chocolate, shaved into curls
>   with a vegetable peeler

1. Line 12 muffin-pan cups with crinkly foil or paper liners and set aside. (I use two 6-muffin pans instead of a single large pan because they're easier to fit into the freezer.)

2. Whisk the condensed milk, evaporated milk, cocoa, Tia Maria, espresso crystals, and vanilla together in a large bowl until smooth. Add the whipped cream and using the whisk, fold in until absolutely smooth. Ladle or pour into the muffin pans, filling to within ⅛ inch of the top. The best implement for pouring is a large plastic measuring cup with a sharply pointed spout. If some of the crinkly cups should push inward as you fill them, insert a small metal skewer or poultry pin into the filling and gently push the crinkly paper back against the side of the muffin-pan cup.

3. Freeze the gelati several hours or until firm. Once the gelati are hard, you can remove them from the muffin pans, pop into a plastic zipper bag, and store in the freezer.

4. To serve, quickly peel the crinkly liners from the gelati, then garnish each, if you like, by drifting with whipped cream and scattering with chocolate curls. I usually shave these directly onto each portion.

FROZEN CHOCOLATE–PEANUT BUTTER CUPS

MAKES 12 SERVINGS

You needn't be a kid to love these chocolate-glazed peanut butter ice cream "muffins." They couldn't be easier to make. Of course, I speed things even more by whizzing the peanut butter portion in a food processor fitted with the metal chopping blade, then whipping the cream there, too (there's no need to wash, rinse, or even wipe the bowl and blade between steps). Here's how I do it: process the condensed milk (minus the one-third cup poured off and reserved), the peanut butter, ½ cup of the heavy cream, and the vanilla four to five seconds until smooth. Scoop into a large bowl, add the remaining 1 cup heavy cream to the machine, and churn ten to twelve seconds until softly whipped. Fold into the peanut butter mixture.

One 14-ounce can sweetened condensed milk
$1/2$ cup creamy peanut butter (measure firmly packed)
$1 1/2$ cups heavy cream
2 teaspoons vanilla extract
3 tablespoons half-and-half or milk
2 tablespoons unsweetened cocoa powder

1. Line 12 muffin-pan cups with crinkly foil or paper liners and set aside. (I use two 6-muffin pans instead of a single large pan because they're easier to fit into the freezer.)
2. Pour ⅓ cup of the condensed milk into a spouted 2-cup measure and set aside. Pour the remaining condensed milk into a large bowl, add the peanut butter, ½ cup of the heavy cream, and the vanilla and whisk hard until smooth (see headnote). Softly whip the remaining 1 cup heavy cream and fold in using the whisk.

3. Ladle or pour into the muffin pans, filling to within ⅛ inch of the top. The best implement for pouring is a large plastic measuring cup with a sharply pointed spout. If some of the crinkly cups should push inward as you fill them, insert a small metal skewer or poultry pin into the filling and gently push the crinkly paper back against the side of the muffin-pan cup.

4. Set the peanut butter cups in the freezer for 30 minutes. Meanwhile, add the half-and-half and cocoa to the ⅓ cup reserved condensed milk and whisk until smooth.

5. Remove the partially frozen peanut butter cups from the freezer and spoon a little of the chocolate mixture on top of each, dividing the total amount equally and smoothing to the edge. Return to the freezer and freeze several hours until firm.

6. To serve, quickly peel the foil or paper liners from the chocolate—peanut butter cups and place on small colorful dessert plates. I don't think that these need any garnish.

FROZEN INDIVIDUAL HAZELNUT MOUSSES

MAKES 12 SERVINGS

So rich, so good, so-o-o quick. And even quicker if you whiz the first three ingredients until smooth in a food processor fitted with the metal chopping blade, scrape into a large bowl, then processor-whip the cream (no need to wash, rinse, or even wipe the bowl and blade). I find this easy dessert elegant enough for a dinner party, and accommodating, too, because it can be made days ahead of time and stored in the freezer.

One 13-ounce jar sweetened chocolate–hazelnut spread (Nutella)
1/2 cup milk
1 teaspoon vanilla extract
2 cups heavy cream, softly whipped
1/4 cup finely chopped lightly toasted hazelnuts (page 16)

1. Line 12 muffin-pan cups with crinkly foil or paper liners and set aside. (Two 6-muffin pans are easier to fit into the freezer than a single large pan.)
2. Scoop the hazelnut spread into a large bowl, add the milk and vanilla, and whisk hard until smooth (see headnote). Fold in the whipped cream using the whisk and continue whisking until smooth.
3. Ladle into the muffin pans, filling to within ⅛ inch of the top, sprinkle 1 teaspoon chopped hazelnuts on top of each, and freeze several hours or until firm. Once the mousses are solidly frozen, you can remove them from the pans and pop into a plastic zipper bag—saves freezer space.
4. To serve, quickly peel the foil or paper liners from the frozen mousses and place on small colorful dessert plates.

4 *I'VE BEEN WORKING* with meatloaves for more than a year now, trying to short-cut the making and the baking. The first is easy. Why settle every time for a can of tomatoes—even old-fashioned tomato sauce—when a gutsy salsa or pasta sauce packs more flavor and eliminates the need to add half a dozen different seasonings?

To simplify things further still, I developed some do-it-yourself herb and spice mixes that can be stirred up in seconds, then kept for months on a cool, dark, dry shelf. I also figured out how to buzz up a big batch of bread crumbs and store them in the freezer so that you don't have to stop and "crumb" five or six slices of bread every time you make a meatloaf.

Trimming meatloaf baking times was harder, however. Raising the oven temperature isn't the answer because the meatloaf will shrink, toughen, and

Meatloaves

dry. A better solution is to shape the meat mixture into a flatter loaf, or better yet two loaves, then to bake them side by side on a jelly-roll pan. Or faster still, to mold them into mini loaves that can be baked in muffin tins.

Even so, certain meatloaves are simply better when baked in a conventional loaf pan at moderate temperature—they're juicier, mellower, and tastier because that slower baking gives their flavors time to mingle and marry. Thus, some of my quick-to-mix meatloaves do require an hour or more in the oven. The good news is that you don't have to babysit them.

You'll note that in addition to specifying meatloaf baking times, I also indicate what the internal temperature of each should be when done—160°F for loaves made with beef, veal, lamb, and pork (165°F if they also contain egg), and 170°F for those made with ground turkey (the "cook-to" temperature recommended by The National Turkey Federation).

EASY ITALIAN MEATLOAF

MAKES 6 TO 8 SERVINGS

My way of trimming meatloaf prep time is to use a gutsy bottled pasta sauce instead of chopped tomatoes or plain tomato sauce because garlic, onions, and a carload of seasonings are already built in—no additional salt needed either. You'll note that this meatloaf contains no egg—it doesn't need any.

TIP: *I keep a stash of soft bread crumbs in the freezer to use in meatloaves and casseroles. It's as easy as buzzing bread odds and ends to crumbs in a food processor and storing in a zipper bag. Or you can follow the directions on page 19.*

1^1/2 cups soft bread crumbs

^{1}/4 cup grated Parmesan (page 18)

1 tablespoon Basic Herb Mix (page 15)

^{1}/2 teaspoon freshly ground black pepper

One 10^1/2-ounce jar puttanesca, arrabbiata, or 1^1/4 cups
    other intensely flavored tomato-based pasta sauce

^{1}/3 cup beef, chicken, or vegetable broth

^{1}/4 cup dry red or white wine

3 tablespoons tomato paste

2 pounds meatloaf mix (1 pound ground beef and ^{1}/2 pound
    each ground pork and veal) or 1 pound each ground beef
    chuck and ground lean beef such as round or sirloin

1. Preheat the oven to 350°F. Coat a 13 × 9 × 2-inch pan with nonstick cooking spray and set aside.

2. Toss the bread crumbs with the Parmesan, herb mix, and pepper in a large bowl, add 1 cup of the puttanesca sauce, the broth, and wine. Stir and let stand 5 minutes.

3. Add the tomato paste and meatloaf mix and using your hands, combine thoroughly. Scoop into the pan and shape into a loaf about 10 inches long, 6 inches wide, and 2 inches high. Spread the remaining puttanesca sauce smoothly on top.

4. Bake the meatloaf in the lower third of the oven until an instant-read meat thermometer inserted in the middle registers 160°F, about 1 hour and 10 minutes.

5. Cool the meatloaf in the pan 15 to 20 minutes, then slice and serve.

QUICK-MIX FIVE-INGREDIENT MEATLOAF

MAKES 6 SERVINGS

Though purists may shriek, I plead guilty to using convenience foods if I'm in a rush to get a meatloaf into the oven. Here, for example, I take advantage of a poultry stuffing mix (and pulse it six to eight times in a food processor), bottled pasta sauce, frozen bell pepper–onion stir-fry strips (processor-pulsed until coarsely chopped), and my own Basic Herb Mix, which significantly trim prep time and eliminate the need for a shelf-load of seasonings. You don't even have to reach for the salt and pepper. This meatloaf goes together fast and bakes in less than an hour.

1 1/2 pounds ground beef, preferably a 50-50 mix of chuck
    and round or sirloin
1 cup poultry stuffing mix (I use a sage-and-onion-flavored
    one)
One 10 1/2-ounce jar pasta sauce with sun-dried tomatoes or
    1 1/4 cups any robust tomato based pasta sauce such as
    puttanesca or arrabbiata
1 1/2 cups solidly frozen bell pepper–onion stir-fry strips,
    coarsely chopped
2 teaspoons Basic Herb Mix (page 15)

1. Preheat the oven to 350°F. Coat a 13 × 9 × 2-inch pan with nonstick cooking spray and aside.
2. Place all meatloaf ingredients in a large bowl, then using your hands, mix together thoroughly. The mixture will be very stiff but the bell pepper strips will exude considerable liquid as the meatloaf bakes so that it's plenty juicy in the end.

3. Place the meat mixture in the pan and shape into a loaf about 10 inches long, 8 inches wide, and 1 to 1½ inches high. Bake in the lower third of the oven until an instant-read meat thermometer inserted in the middle registers 160°F, 50 to 55 minutes.

4. Cool the meatloaf in the pan 15 minutes, pour off all drippings (these are mostly fat), slice, and serve. I slice the loaf right in the pan—saves an extra step.

BARBECUED BEEF LOAF

MAKES 4 TO 6 SERVINGS

Few meatloaves are easier than this one—or better. You can substitute 1¼ cups coarsely crumbled corn flakes for the cornbread stuffing mix (I just crumble the cereal as I drop it into the measure) and mix in one large egg. For this meatloaf, I prefer a 50-50 mix of lean ground chuck and sirloin, but the 90 percent lean ground beef that most supermarkets sell is fine, too.

1 pound lean ground beef

6 scallions, trimmed and thinly sliced (include some green tops)

1 cup bottled barbecue sauce (as hot and spicy as you like) plus more for serving, if desired

1 cup cornbread stuffing mix

2 large garlic cloves, finely chopped, or $^{1}/_{2}$ teaspoon garlic powder

2 teaspoons Basic Herb Mix (page 15)

$^{1}/_{4}$ teaspoon salt

1. Preheat the oven to 350°F. Coat a jelly-roll pan with nonstick cooking spray; set aside.
2. Using your hands, mix the beef, scallions, ¾ cup of the barbecue sauce, the stuffing mix, garlic, herb mix, and salt thoroughly in a large bowl. Scoop onto the pan and shape into a 9 × 7 × 2-inch oval. Spread with the remaining ¼ cup barbecue sauce.
3. Bake in the lower third of the oven until the loaf is richly browned and an instant-read meat thermometer inserted into the middle registers 160°F, 50 to 55 minutes.
4. Let the meatloaf rest at room temperature 10 minutes, then slice and serve. Pass extra barbecue sauce, if you like.

MUFFALETTA LOAF

MAKES 8 SERVINGS

This meatloaf is plenty spicy thanks to the pork sausage and bottled muffaletta—an intensely flavorful New Orleans relish loaded with chopped dried tomatoes and olives.

1¹/2 pounds ground beef (a 50-50 mix of lean ground chuck
  and sirloin)
¹/2 pound pork sausage meat
1 large yellow onion, coarsely chopped or 1¹/2 cups solidly
  frozen chopped onion
1 cup ¹/2-inch cubes firm white bread
1 cup bottled muffaletta relish
1 tablespoon Basic Herb Mix (page 15)

1. Preheat the oven to 375°F. Coat a jelly-roll pan with nonstick cooking spray and set aside.
2. Using your hands, mix all ingredients thoroughly in a large bowl. Scoop into the pan and shape into a round loaf about 10 inches across and 1½ inches high. Score the top of the loaf into 8 wedges.
3. Bake in the lower third of the oven until an instant-read meat thermometer inserted in the middle of the loaf registers 160°F, 40 to 45 minutes. Let the loaf rest 10 minutes.
4. Transfer to a heated round platter, cut into wedges, and serve.

BEEF LOAF WITH SWEET ITALIAN SAUSAGES, LEMON, AND ANCHOVIES

MAKES 8 TO 10 SERVINGS

Once while traveling about Sicily, I was served a meatloaf very much like this one in a little mom-and-pop restaurant in Agrigento. I began scribbling notes, trying to crack the recipe, and as soon as I returned to New York, I translated those notes into a delicious meatloaf. This is a faster version although the slow baking time remains the same. The meatloaf would cook faster at higher oven heat but it would also toughen and dry. At least you don't have to hang around and prod or baste the meatloaf. It's self-basting. Leftovers, you'll be pleased to know, make superb sandwiches, especially if you use a good, chewy Italian bread, slice it half an inch thick, and brush lightly with olive oil. For lettuce, I use radicchio or arugula.

1¹/₂ pounds lean ground beef chuck

1 pound sweet Italian sausages, removed from their casings

2 cups soft white bread crumbs (page 19)

8 large scallions, trimmed and finely chopped (include some green tops)

2 large garlic cloves, minced

1¹/₂ cups canned crushed tomatoes with their liquid

¹/₂ cup dry white wine such as a pinot grigio

2 large eggs

2 tablespoons anchovy paste

1 tablespoon Basic Herb Mix (page 15)

1 tablespoon finely grated lemon zest

1 teaspoon coarsely crushed fennel seeds

¹/₂ teaspoon freshly ground black pepper

3 to 5 lemon twists

3 to 5 frilly finocchio (fennel) tops or sprigs of arugula

1. Preheat the oven to 350°F. Lightly coat a 9 × 5 × 3-inch loaf pan with nonstick cooking spray and set aside.

2. Place all ingredients in a large mixing bowl, and using your hands, mix together well. Pack into the loaf pan, mounding the mixture slightly in the center.

3. Set on a baking sheet and bake on the middle oven shelf until richly browned and an instant-read meat thermometer inserted in the middle of the loaf reads 165°F, about 1 hour and 30 to 40 minutes.

4. Remove the meatloaf from the oven and cool in the upright pan for 20 minutes. Pour off all drippings, then turn the loaf out onto a heated platter and garnish, if you like, with twists of lemon and frilly finocchio (fennel) tops. Cut into slices about ¾ inch thick and serve.

GRANDMA JOHNSON'S BEST MEATLOAF

MAKES 6 TO 8 SERVINGS

My mother grew up on this meatloaf, my brother and I grew up on this meatloaf, and it's the standard by which I judge all others. I have, however, made a few changes in Grandma's recipe, mostly to speed things up: six large scallions (quickly trimmed and chopped as a bunch) instead of a yellow onion, which must be peeled and chopped; a frozen stash of soft white bread crumbs (Grandma lived pre-freezer); fat-free evaporated milk in place of fresh whole milk (I like its mellowing effect and slightly caramel flavor), and finally bottled crumbled bacon or the soy equivalent if I don't have a few slices of crisply cooked bacon on hand. I also processor-chop the scallions, green pepper, and celery together, pulsing to just the right degree of chop. What hasn't changed is the addition of baking powder. Grandma always added a hefty pinch to her meatloaf. "To make it lighter," she once told me. I like this meatloaf better warm than oven-hot, which gives it a chance to firm up. I also like it cold—especially in sandwiches.

3 cups soft white bread crumbs (page 19)

Two 5-ounce cans fat-free evaporated milk

1$1/2$ pounds lean ground beef

$1/4$ cup finely crumbled crisp bacon (about 2 slices)

6 large scallions, trimmed and coarsely chopped

1 small green bell pepper, cored, seeded, and coarsely chopped

1 large celery rib, trimmed and coarsely chopped

$1/2$ cup ketchup

1 teaspoon baking powder

$1/2$ teaspoon salt

$1/2$ teaspoon freshly ground black pepper

5 slices uncooked lean bacon

1. Preheat the oven to 350°F. Coat a 9 × 5 × 3-inch pan with nonstick cooking spray and set aside.
2. Place the bread crumbs in a large bowl, pour the milk evenly on top, and allow to soak while you prep the other ingredients.
3. Add all remaining ingredients to the bowl and mix thoroughly using your hands. Scoop the mixture into the pan, mounding slightly in the center.
4. Bake in the lower third of the oven for over 20 minutes. Remove from the oven and raise the temperature to 375°F. Lay the bacon strips lengthwise on top of the loaf, overlapping slightly and tucking the ends down against the pan with a thin-blade spatula (this helps keep the bacon from shrinking).
5. Return the meatloaf to the oven and bake until the bacon is nicely browned and an instant-read meat thermometer inserted in the middle of the loaf registers 160°F, 35 to 40 minutes.
6. Cool the meatloaf in the pan 20 minutes, pour off all drippings (these are mostly fat), slice, and serve. I do this right in the pan because this loaf is unusually moist and tender. The first slice is always difficult to remove. It helps, I find, to set the pan on its side and ease each slice out with a small, thin-blade spatula.

AUNT FLORENCE'S BEEF AND SAUSAGE LOAF

MAKES 8 SERVINGS

My mother's only sister was my favorite aunt—partly because she lived on a big farm in central Illinois, but mostly because she was so energetic and kind. Aunt Florence had no daughters, so whenever I went to visit in summer, I became her daughter for two, sometimes three or even four weeks. My greatest joys were gathering eggs, milking cows, and separating the cream. I even helped Aunt Florence make sausage, some of which went into this husky meatloaf. It does take a while to bake, but it's quick to mix and needs no attention once it's in the oven.

1¹/2 pounds lean ground beef chuck

1 pound pork sausage meat (not too fat)

1 cup quick-cooking rolled oats

1 medium yellow onion, moderately coarsely chopped

³/4 cup tomato juice (Aunt Florence made and canned her own)

¹/4 cup water

¹/4 cup tomato ketchup

2 large eggs

1 tablespoon prepared spicy brown mustard

1 teaspoon salt

¹/4 teaspoon freshly ground black pepper

1. Preheat the oven to 350°F. Coat a 9 × 5 × 3-inch loaf pan well with nonstick cooking spray and aside.
2. Place all ingredients in a large bowl and mix thoroughly with your hands. Scoop into the pan and shape into a loaf, mounding it slightly in the center.

3. Bake the meatloaf on the middle oven rack until nicely browned and an instant-read thermometer inserted into the middle of it registers 165°F, about 1½ hours.

4. Remove the meatloaf from the oven and cool 20 minutes. Pour off any accumulated drippings—these can either be spooned over each portion or frozen and used to make soup or stew another day. Slice the meatloaf about ¾ inch thick—Aunt Florence always did this right in the pan—and serve.

LINDSTROM LOAF

I've always loved beef à la Lindstrom, those Swedish "burgers" plumped with finely diced beets and potatoes. So why not a Lindstrom meatloaf? To save time, I use canned, pickled beets and baked potatoes, which require no peeling. Baking potatoes takes time, it's true, but all you have to do is set them in a 400°F oven and forget them for an hour. Even faster, microwave the potatoes eight to ten minutes on HIGH. But pierce them first lest they explode.

Because the amount of moisture in potatoes varies significantly, you may need as much as three-quarters cup of milk to make the potato "frosting" a good spreading consistency—my niece Linda did when she recently made this recipe. And yet I've rarely used more than four tablespoons. My best advice is to add the milk about two tablespoons at a time and continue just until the potatoes are soft enough to swirl over the meatloaf.

MEATLOAF

2 medium Idaho potatoes (about 1 1/4 pounds), baked until tender (see headnote)

3/4 cup well-drained sliced pickled beets

3/4 pound lean ground beef

1/2 cup sour cream (use "light," if you like)

4 large scallions, trimmed and finely chopped

2 tablespoons well-drained dill pickle relish

1 tablespoon well-drained small capers

1 tablespoon finely snipped fresh dill or 1/2 teaspoon dried dill weed

1/2 teaspoon salt

1/4 teaspoon freshly ground black pepper

> **1 mashed, baked medium Idaho potato (about 10 ounces,
> reserved from the meatloaf above)**
> **1 tablespoon butter, softened**
> **4 to 6 tablespoons milk (just enough for good spreading
> consistency)**
> **Salt and freshly ground black pepper to taste**

1. Preheat the oven to 350°F. Coat a jelly-roll pan with nonstick cooking spray and aside.

2. MEATLOAF: Scoop the potato flesh into a large bowl and mash with a potato masher until light and fluffy. Transfer half of the mashed potato to a 2-quart measure and reserve for the frosting. Add the beets to the potatoes in the bowl and mash until the texture of coarse meal. Add all remaining meatloaf ingredients and mix well with your hands.

3. Scoop the mixture onto the jelly-roll pan and shape into a loaf about 6 inches long, 3 inches wide, and 1½ inches high. Bake in the lower third of the oven for 20 minutes.

4. "FROSTING": While the meatloaf is baking, whisk the butter with the reserved mashed potatoes until fluffy. Whisk in 3 tablespoons of the milk and if too stiff to spread, continue adding milk until the frosting is good spreading consistency. Season to taste with salt and pepper.

5. Take the meatloaf from the oven and raise the temperature to 375°F. Swirl the frosting over the meatloaf. Return to the oven and bake until tipped with brown and an instant-read thermometer stuck in the middle of the loaf registers 160°F, about 30 minutes.

6. Cool the meatloaf in the pan 15 minutes, slice slant-wise like London broil, and serve.

BEEF 'N' BULGUR LOAVES
WITH WILD MUSHROOMS AND SOUR CREAM SAUCE
MAKES 6 TO 8 SERVINGS

The only time-consuming part of this recipe is soaking the dried mushrooms, but that job can be done ahead of time and the rehydrated mushrooms refrigerated until needed. For this recipe, I use frozen small white onions because I like their intense flavor. I chop them in a food processor along with all of the seasonings, turning two tasks into one. Although I rarely use onion flakes, parsley flakes, or garlic powder, I offer them as options for those who must cook dinner on a deadline.

NOTE: *The instant bulgur available to most of us is sold as tabbouleh with a separate packet of seasoning. Use the tabbouleh but save the seasoning for another day.*

MEATLOAVES

Two 1/2-ounce envelopes dried chanterelles or other wild
mushrooms (but not the large and leathery porcini,
which must be chopped)

3 cups boiling water

1 cup instant bulgur (tabbouleh)

1 1/2 pounds ground beef, preferably a 50-50 mix of chuck
and round or sirloin

1/2 cup grated Parmesan (page 18)

One 1-pound package frozen small white onions, partially
thawed, or 1/3 cup onion flakes

1 large garlic clove or 1/2 teaspoon garlic powder

1/4 cup flat-leaf parsley leaves or 2 tablespoons parsley
flakes

2 teaspoons Basic Herb Mix (page 15)

1 1/2 teaspoons salt

1/2 teaspoon freshly ground black pepper

Meatloaf drippings, if any

^{1}/2 cup reserved mushroom soaking liquid

1^1/4 cups sour cream, at room temperature (use "light,"
     if you like)

1. MEATLOAVES: Crumble the dried mushrooms in the unopened envelopes, then open, drop into a 2-cup measure, add 2 cups of the boiling water, and let stand for 30 minutes. When the mushrooms have soaked 25 minutes, place the bulgur in a second bowl, add the remaining 1 cup boiling water, and let stand 5 minutes.
2. When ready to proceed, preheat the oven to 350°F. Coat a 13 × 9 × 2-inch pan with nonstick cooking spray and set aside.
3. Drain the mushrooms in a coffee filter–lined sieve set over a 1-quart measure. Rinse the mushrooms and place in a large bowl along with 1 cup soaking liquid; reserve the remaining soaking liquid. Also add the bulgur to the bowl (it will have absorbed all of its water) along with the ground beef and Parmesan.
4. If using the partially thawed onions, pulse 10 to 12 times with all remaining meatloaf ingredients in a food processor fitted with the metal chopping blade or until finely chopped. Add to the bowl and using your hands, mix everything together thoroughly. If using onion flakes, simply add to the bowl along with all remaining ingredients.
5. Place the meat mixture in the pan and shape into two loaves, each about 8 inches long, 5 inches wide, and 2 inches high.
6. Bake in the lower third of the oven until an instant-read meat thermometer inserted in the middle of a loaf, registers 160°F, about 1 hour. Let the meatloaves rest 10 minutes, then transfer to a heated platter.

7. SAUCE: Drain any hot meatloaf drippings into a 1-quart measure. Pour the reserved mushroom liquid into the baking pan, set over moderate heat, and cook and stir 1 to 2 minutes, scraping up all browned bits. Pour into the measure and whisk into the drippings. Cool 5 minutes, then whisk in the sour cream. If there are no drippings, simply cool the mushroom deglazing liquid 5 minutes and whisk in the sour cream. Taste for salt and add as needed.

8. Slice the meatloaves and spoon a little of the gravy over each portion.

BEEF CARBONNADE LOAF

MAKES 4 TO 6 SERVINGS

I have always loved the Belgian beef–beer stew called carbonnade à la flamande and wanted to work up an easy meatloaf that captured its flavor. The best accompaniments? Boiled tiny redskin potatoes (no need to peel) and roasted asparagus.

1 pound ground beef (a 50-50 mix of lean ground chuck and
    sirloin)
1 large yellow onion, coarsely chopped
1 cup coarsely crumbled salted pretzels (80 to 90 thin,
    3-inch sticks)
$^3/_4$ cup flat beer
2 garlic cloves, finely chopped
1 teaspoon dried thyme leaves
$^1/_4$ teaspoon salt
$^1/_4$ teaspoon freshly grated nutmeg

1. Preheat the oven to 375°F. Coat a 13 × 9 × 2-inch pan with nonstick cooking spray and set aside.
2. Using your hands mix all ingredients thoroughly in a large bowl. Place the meat mixture in the pan and shape into a loaf about 8 inches long, 6 inches wide, and 1½ inches high.
3. Bake in the lower third of the oven until an instant-read meat thermometer inserted in the middle of the loaf, registers 160°F, 35 to 40 minutes.
4. Let the meatloaf rest 10 minutes, ease onto a heated platter, and serve.

LIGHTLY CURRIED VEAL (OR TURKEY) AND CABBAGE LOAF WITH YOGURT GRAVY

MAKES 8 TO 10 SERVINGS

You might think cabbage an odd vegetable to curry and an even odder one to bake into meatloaf. Not at all. The recipe I liked best when I spent several months in India was curried cabbage, a fast stir-fry. Of course the meat used in India is mostly lamb (or fish or fowl). Never beef, veal, or pork. Chop the cabbage, green pepper, and onion in tandem in the food processor. Also mince the garlic along with all seasonings, pulsing to just the texture you want.

MEATLOAF

1 pound ground veal or turkey (not too fat)

¹/2 pound ground pork (not too fat)

2 cups soft white bread crumbs (page 19)

6 ounces cabbage, trimmed, cored, and cut into 1-inch chunks

1 medium yellow onion, peeled and cut into 1-inch chunks

1 small green bell pepper, cored, seeded, and cut into 1-inch chunks

2 large garlic cloves, peeled

¹/4 cup mango chutney

4 teaspoons curry powder

1 tablespoon Basic Herb Mix (page 15)

1¹/2 teaspoons salt

3 large eggs

One 8-ounce can tomato sauce

1/2 cup water

1/2 cup meatloaf drippings or drippings plus enough chicken broth to total 1/2 cup

1 cup plain yogurt, at room temperature (do not use low-fat)

One 3-ounce package cream cheese, at room temperature

1. Preheat the oven to 350°F. Lightly coat a jelly-roll pan with nonstick cooking spray and set aside.

2. MEATLOAF: Place the veal, pork, and bread crumbs in a large mixing bowl and set aside. Equip the food processor with the metal chopping blade, add the cabbage, onion, and bell pepper and pulse briskly until the texture of finely cut slaw. Add to the mixing bowl.

3. Add the garlic, chutney, curry powder, herb mix, and salt to the processor and churn until smooth—8 to 10 seconds. Quickly pulse in the eggs and tomato sauce—you don't want to purée them, merely to combine. Add to the bowl, then using your hands, mix everything together well. Scoop the mixture into the pan and shape into a loaf about 10 inches long, 8 inches wide, and 2 inches high, packing firmly and mounding slightly in the center.

4. Bake on the middle oven shelf until richly browned and an instant-read meat thermometer inserted in the middle of the loaf reads 165°F (170°F for ground turkey), about 1 hour. Remove the meatloaf from the oven and let stand 15 minutes, then gently ease onto a piece of heavy-duty aluminum foil. Pour off and reserve the pan drippings.

5. GRAVY: Set the jelly-roll pan over two stovetop burners set at moderate heat, add the water, and scrape and stir, loosening the browned bits. Pour into a 1-quart measure, add the reserved drippings, yogurt, and cream cheese and whisk until smooth.

6. To serve, slice the loaf about 3/4 inch thick. Overlap the slices on a heated platter and spoon some of the gravy down the middle. Sprig with parsley, if you like, and add a few clusters of grape tomatoes. Pass the remaining gravy separately.

VEAL (OR TURKEY), HAM, AND MUSHROOM LOAF WITH HORSERADISH SAUCE

MAKES 8 TO 10 SERVINGS

You can substitute ground turkey for veal but use a 50-50 mix of light and dark meat. To save time, I pulse the crackers to crumbs in a food processor, then processor-chop the mushrooms, onion, and green pepper together—eight to ten staccato pulses are all it takes.

2 pounds ground veal (not too lean) or turkey

$1/2$ pound ground ham

$2^1/2$ cups moderately coarsely crushed soda crackers

1 cup milk

2 large eggs

$1/4$ cup tomato ketchup

$1/4$ cup prepared horseradish

$1^1/2$ teaspoons salt

2 tablespoons unsalted butter

One 10-ounce package sliced white mushrooms, coarsely chopped

1 large yellow onion, coarsely chopped

$1/2$ small green pepper, cored, seeded, and coarsely chopped

4 slices double-smoked or deeply smoky bacon

2 cups room temperature sour cream blended with $1/4$ cup prepared horseradish (sauce)

1. Preheat the oven to 350°F. Lightly spritz a jelly-roll pan with nonstick cooking spray and set aside.

2. Place the veal, ham, cracker crumbs, milk, eggs, ketchup, horseradish, and salt in a large mixing bowl and set aside.

3. Melt the butter in a large heavy skillet over moderate heat, add the mushrooms, onion, and green pepper and sauté, stirring occasionally, until the mushrooms release their juices and these evaporate, 5 to 8 minutes. Tip all into the mixing bowl, and using your hands, mix everything together well. Scoop the mixture into the baking pan and shape into a loaf about 12 inches long, 9 inches wide, and 2 inches high, mounding it slightly in the center. Lay the bacon strips on top, arranging them on the bias and spacing evenly.

4. Bake the meatloaf on the middle oven shelf until richly browned and an instant-read meat thermometer inserted in the middle registers 165°F (170°F for ground turkey), 45 to 50 minutes. Remove the meatloaf from the oven and let rest for 15 minutes.

5. To serve, slice the meatloaf about ¾ inch thick. Overlap the slices on a heated platter and spoon some of the sauce down the middle. Pass any remaining sauce separately.

COFFEE-BASTED LAMB LOAF WITH DILL PICKLE SAUCE

MAKES 4 TO 6 SERVINGS

In Sweden morning coffee is used to baste a roast, making the meat unusually flavorful. I've adopted a similar technique for this quick and easy lamb loaf. I've also substituted scallions for yellow onion because they have punchier flavor and are quicker to prepare. While the scallions are still bunched, trim off the roots and all but about two inches of the green tops. Wash them quickly, then re-bunch, and slice thin or chop. Because the loaf and sauce both call for half a cup of coarsely chopped dill pickles, chop them all at once—two medium-large pickles should be enough.

LAMB LOAF

1 pound ground lamb (not too lean)

$1^1/2$ cups soft white bread crumbs (page 19)

6 scallions, trimmed and thinly sliced or coarsely chopped
   (include some green tops)

$1/2$ cup coarsely chopped dill pickle (see headnote)

$1/3$ cup coarsely chopped fresh dill or 1 teaspoon dried dill
   weed

$1/3$ cup plain low-fat yogurt

$1/2$ teaspoon salt

$1/4$ teaspoon cracked black pepper

$1/4$ cup strong coffee (leftover is fine)

SAUCE

$1/4$ cup strong coffee (leftover is fine)

$1/2$ cup sour cream (use "light," if you like)

$1/4$ cup mayonnaise (use "light," if you like)

$1/2$ cup coarsely chopped dill pickle

Salt, as needed

1. Preheat the oven to 375°F. Coat a jelly-roll pan with nonstick cooking spray and set aside.
2. LOAF: Place the lamb, bread crumbs, scallions, dill pickle, dill, yogurt, salt, and pepper in a large bowl, then using your hands, mix well. Scoop into the pan and shape into a flat 8 × 6 × 2-inch oval. Score the top criss-cross fashion, making the cuts about 1 inch apart. Drizzle the coffee evenly on top.
3. Bake in the lower third of the oven until richly browned and an instant-read meat thermometer inserted in the middle of the loaf registers 160°F, 50 to 55 minutes.
4. Using two spatulas, ease the loaf onto a heated platter, and let rest 10 minutes.
5. SAUCE: While the loaf is resting, skim any fat and blackened bits from the pan; add the coffee and stir, scraping up the richly flavored browned bits on the bottom of the pan. Place the sour cream and mayonnaise in a small bowl, then gradually whisk in the coffee mixture. Fold in the pickle, taste for salt and add, if needed.
6. Slice the lamb loaf and ladle a little of the sauce over each portion.

CROFTER'S LAMB LOAF WITH OATMEAL AND APPLE

MAKES 8 SERVINGS

A hearty Scottish meatloaf that can be mixed in a jif, then shoved into the oven to bake while you go about your business. To save time, I processor-chop the scallions and apple together.

1 cup quick-cooking rolled oats

$1/2$ cup apple cider

2 pounds lean ground lamb shoulder

6 medium scallions, trimmed and coarsely chopped (include some green tops)

1 large Granny Smith apple, peeled, cored, and coarsely chopped

1 extra-large egg

2 teaspoons Basic Herb Mix (page 15)

2 teaspoons salt

$1/2$ teaspoon freshly grated nutmeg

$1/4$ teaspoon freshly ground black pepper

1. Preheat the oven to 350°F. Lightly coat an $8^{1/2} \times 4^{1/2} \times 2^{3/4}$-inch loaf pan with nonstick cooking spray and set aside.
2. Place the oats in a large mixing bowl, pour the apple cider evenly over them, and let stand 10 minutes. Add all remaining ingredients and mix well using your hands. Pack into the loaf pan, mounding slightly in the center.

3. Bake on the middle oven shelf until richly browned and an instant-read meat thermometer inserted in the middle of the loaf reads 165°F, about 1 hour.
4. Remove the meatloaf from the oven and let stand 15 minutes. Pour off all accumulated drippings. These can be spooned over the meatloaf slices or frozen and used later in gravies, soups, or stews.
5. Loosen the meatloaf around the edge with a thin-blade metal spatula and turn out onto a heated platter. Slice about ½ inch thick and serve, topping each portion, if you like, with a spoonful of the drippings.

BOBOTIE

I first tasted this curried Cape Malay lamb loaf when I was on assignment in South Africa. This is a vastly simplified version. Quicker, too, because I do the chopping in a food processor.

LOAF

2 large garlic cloves

One 1-inch chunk fresh ginger, peeled

3 cups solidly frozen bell pepper–onion stir-fry mix

1¹/₂ tablespoons curry powder

1 teaspoon Three-Spice Mix (page 13)

2 tablespoons peanut or vegetable oil

1¹/₂ pounds ground lamb (not too lean)

1¹/₂ cups soft white bread crumbs (page 19)

¹/₂ cup golden seedless raisins

¹/₂ cup milk or fat-free evaporated milk

1 teaspoon salt

¹/₄ teaspoon freshly ground black pepper

TOPPING

³/₄ cup milk

1 large egg

¹/₄ teaspoon salt

1. Preheat the oven to 375°F. Lightly coat a 9-inch round layer cake pan with nonstick spray and set aside.

2. L O A F : Finely chop the garlic and ginger together in a food processor fitted with the metal chopping blade by churning 5 seconds. Scrape the work bowl, add the stir-fry mix, curry powder, and spice mix and pulse briskly 8 to 10 times until coarsely chopped.

3. Heat the oil in a large heavy skillet over high heat, add the chopped mixture, and stir-fry until tender and touched with brown, 6 to 8 minutes.

4. Transfer to a large mixing bowl. Add the lamb, bread crumbs, raisins, milk, salt, and pepper and mix thoroughly using your hands. Pat all into the greased pan, then push the meat mixture about ½ inch up the sides of the pan, forming a little rim.

5. Bake the loaf on the middle oven shelf for 30 minutes.

6. T O P P I N G : While the loaf is baking, whisk the milk, egg, and salt together until smooth. Set aside.

7. Remove the meatloaf from the oven, and drain off any drippings, reserving, if you like, to use another time for gravy, sauce, soup, or stew. Pour the topping into the hollow in the middle of the loaf and bake until it sets and an instant-read meat thermometer inserted in the middle of the loaf reads 160°F, about 30 minutes.

8. Let the bobotie rest 5 minutes, then using two spatulas, ease onto a heated round platter. Cut into wedges and serve.

KIBBEH

This recipe comes from the guide who showed me about Lebanon many years ago. Or rather the long-winded original does. This is my streamlined food processor update. Lebanese women still pound the lamb and bulgur to paste by hand. And chop the onions and garlic by hand, too.

1^1/2 cups instant bulgur (tabbouleh)
1^1/2 cups boiling water
2 medium yellow onions, cut into slim wedges
4 large garlic cloves
2 pounds finely ground lamb (not too lean)
2 teaspoons salt
2 teaspoons Five-Spice Mix (page 14)
^{3}/4 cup dried currants
^{1}/2 cup pine nuts, coarsely chopped
2 cups plain low-fat yogurt (optional)
^{1}/3 cup coarsely chopped mint leaves (optional)

1. Preheat the oven to 350°F. Lightly coat a 13 × 9 × 2-inch pan with nonstick spray and set aside. Combine the bulgur and boiling water in a medium bowl; set aside for 10 minutes or until all water is absorbed.
2. Meanwhile, pulse the onions and garlic 8 to 10 times in a food processor fitted with the metal chopping blade until coarsely chopped. Scoop out ²/₃ cup and reserve.
3. Add the soaked bulgur to the processor along with half each of the lamb and salt and pulse 10 to 12 times. Scrape the work bowl, then pulse 10 to 12 times more until thick and paste-like. Pat half of this mixture over the bottom of the pan.

4. Combine the remaining ground lamb and salt with the spice mix, currants, and reserved chopped onion mixture in the bowl in which you soaked the bulgur. Pat smoothly on top of the layer in the pan, then pat the remaining paste-like lamb–bulgur mixture into a third smooth layer. Score in a diamond pattern, spacing the cuts about 1 inch apart. Sprinkle the pine nuts evenly over all and press firmly into the meat.

5. Bake on the middle oven shelf until lightly browned and an instant-read meat thermometer inserted into the middle of the loaf registers 160°F, about 45 minutes.

6. Cut into large rectangles and serve. Top each portion, if you like, with yogurt and a scattering of freshly chopped mint.

SPICY HAM LOAF

Many supermarkets now sell ground pork but few, I've discovered, also sell ground ham or will do the job for you. If you have a food processor, no problem. Simply trim the ham of excess fat and connective tissue, cut into one-inch cubes, and pulse until moderately finely ground. Without a processor, you'll have to put the ham through an old-fashioned meat grinder, or worse, hand-chop it. Reason enough for adding a food processor to your kitchen.

3/4 pound ground fully cooked smoked ham

3/4 pound ground pork

1 cup soft white bread crumbs (page 19) or 1/2 cup
    cornbread stuffing mix

1/2 cup orange juice

1 medium yellow onion, coarsely chopped, or 3 tablespoons
    onion flakes

1/4 cup coarsely chopped flat-leaf parsley or 2 tablespoons
    parsley flakes

1/2 cup mustard pickle relish

1 1/2 teaspoons Basic Herb Mix (page 15)

1 1/2 teaspoons Three-Spice Mix (page 13)

1. Preheat the oven to 375°F. Coat a 13 × 9 × 2-inch pan with nonstick cooking spray and set aside.
2. Place all ingredients in a large bowl and mix thoroughly, using your hands. Scoop into the pan and shape into a loaf about 10 inches long, 7 inches wide, and 1½ inches high.

3. Bake in the lower third of the oven until nicely browned and an instant-read meat thermometer inserted in the middle of the loaf registers 160°F, 35 to 40 minutes.

4. Let rest 20 minutes, slice, and serve. Or chill well and serve cold. Delicious as is but better yet topped with Sour Cream–Mustard–Horseradish Sauce, which follows.

Sour Cream–Mustard–Horseradish Sauce

MAKES ABOUT 1 CUP

3/4 cup sour cream

2 tablespoons Dijon mustard, preferably whole-grain

2 tablespoons prepared horseradish

1 tablespoon well-drained small capers

1 tablespoon milk or as needed to thin to the consistency of medium white sauce

1 tablespoon freshly snipped dill or 1/2 teaspoon dried dill weed

Whisk all ingredients together and serve over Spicy Ham Loaf, which precedes. Also delicious over boiled or baked ham.

SWEET-AND-SOUR HAM LOAF
WITH DRIED APPLES AND SWEET POTATO

MAKES 8 TO 10 SERVINGS

The food processor makes short shrift of this recipe because it chops the sweet potatoes and dried apples. It will also grind the ham if you're unable to buy it pre-ground or your butcher is unwilling to do the job for you. I find this sweet-sour ham loaf a good party dish because it can be made in advance, even plated ahead of time, and served cold. Accompany with additional cranberry sauce or, if you prefer, with Sour Cream–Mustard–Horseradish Sauce (page 216).

1 medium sweet potato (about 8 ounces), peeled and cut
  into 1 1/2-inch chunks
One 5-ounce bag dried apples
1/2 pound ground fully cooked smoked ham or if you're
  unable to buy ground ham, 1/2 pound trimmed ham,
  cut into 1-inch chunks
1/2 pound ground pork
1 cup frozen chopped onions (no need to thaw)
1 cup apple juice
2 large eggs
1/2 cup old-fashioned rolled oats
1 1/2 teaspoons Basic Herb Mix (page 15)
1/2 teaspoon Five-Spice Mix (page 14)
One 8-ounce can jellied cranberry sauce

1. Preheat the oven to 375°F. Coat a 13 × 9 × 2-inch pan with nonstick cooking spray and set aside.

2. Pulse the sweet potato and dried apples in a food processor fitted with the metal chopping blade until moderately finely chopped—10 to 12 pulses should do it. Tip the sweet potato mixture into a large bowl.

3. If you've been unable to buy ground ham, drop the chunks into the food processor (no need to wash or wipe the bowl and blade) and pulse quickly until moderately finely ground—10 to 12 pulses is about right.

4. Add the ground ham, pork, onions, apple juice, eggs, oats, herb and spice mixes, and half the cranberry sauce to the sweet potato mixture and mix thoroughly using your hands. Scoop into the pan and shape into a loaf about 12 inches long, 8 inches wide, and 1½ inches high. Score the top of the loaf in a diagonal diamond pattern just the way you would score a baked ham.

5. Bake in the lower third of the oven for 35 minutes. Meanwhile, melt the remaining cranberry sauce over low heat or by microwaving 1½ to 2 minutes on HIGH. Spread the melted cranberry sauce over the loaf and return to the oven until richly browned and an instant-read meat thermometer inserted in the middle of the loaf registers 165°F, 10 to 15 minutes longer.

6. Let the ham loaf rest 15 minutes, then slice, and serve. Or, if you prefer, chill and serve cold.

CURRANT-AND-MUSTARD GLAZED HAM LOAF WITH BROWN OR WHITE RICE

MAKES 6 TO 8 SERVINGS

The meatloaf to make when you have leftover rice—either home-cooked or Chinese take-out. It's also a good way to use up the last of a big baked ham.

> 1¹/2 pounds ground cooked ham
>
> 1¹/2 cups firmly packed, unseasoned, cooked brown or white rice
>
> 1¹/2 cups soft white bread crumbs (page 19; do not pack into the measure)
>
> One 12-ounce can fat-free evaporated milk
>
> 3 large eggs
>
> 6 large scallions, trimmed and minced (include some green tops)
>
> 2 teaspoons Basic Herb Mix (page 15)
>
> 1¹/2 teaspoons dry mustard
>
> ¹/2 cup red currant jelly blended with ¹/3 cup prepared yellow mustard (glaze)

1. Preheat the oven to 350°F. Line a 13 × 9 × 2-inch baking pan with aluminum foil, then lightly spritz the foil with nonstick cooking spray; set aside.
2. Place all ingredients except the currant—mustard glaze in a large bowl and mix thoroughly with your hands. Scoop into the pan and shape into a loaf about 10 inches long, 5 inches wide, and 3 inches high.

3. Bake the meatloaf on the middle oven rack for 50 minutes; remove from the oven and spread with the glaze. Return to the oven and bake until glistening and an instant-read thermometer thrust into the middle of the loaf registers 165°F, 15 to 20 minutes longer.

4. Remove the meatloaf from the oven and cool 20 minutes before slicing.

A GOOD BASIC TURKEY (OR VEAL) LOAF

MAKES 4 TO 6 SERVINGS

It's best to use a combination of dark and light turkey meat for this recipe because the light is too lean to produce a moist and tender loaf. The veal you want is pale, milk-fed veal, not baby beef.

3/4 pound ground turkey (preferably a 50-50 mix of dark and
   light meat) or ground veal shoulder
3/4 pound turkey Italian sausage, removed from skins
1 medium yellow onion, moderately coarsely chopped
1/2 cup milk
1/3 cup soft white bread crumbs (page 19)
1/4 cup ketchup or chili sauce
1 garlic clove, finely chopped
2 teaspoons Basic Herb Mix (page 15)

1. Preheat the oven to 350°F. Coat an 8½ × 4½ × 2¾-inch loaf pan with nonstick cooking spray and set aside.
2. Using your hands, mix all ingredients together well in a large bowl. Pack the mixture into the pan and bake in the lower third of the oven until an instant-read meat thermometer inserted into the middle of the loaf registers 170°F (160°F for veal), 45 to 50 minutes.
3. Let the turkey loaf rest in the upright pan 15 minutes, then turn out on a heated platter, slice, and serve.

CURRIED TURKEY (OR VEAL) LOAF

MAKES 4 TO 6 SERVINGS

One of my pet short-cuts is to use instant rice in meatloaves, either the white or the brown, because it can go in as is. Another time-saver is the frozen bell pepper–onion stir-fry mix sold in most supermarkets. I don't thaw it because it chops much more crisply when solidly frozen. To save additional time, I do the chopping in a food processor fitted with the metal chopping blade and at the same time, incorporate all of the seasonings. A few seconds is all it takes.

3 cups solidly frozen bell pepper–onion stir-fry mix

1/3 cup mango chutney

3 to 4 teaspoons curry powder (depending upon how fond
   you are of curry)

1 tablespoon Basic Herb Mix (page 15)

1/2 teaspoon salt

1/2 teaspoon freshly ground black pepper

1 pound ground turkey or ground veal shoulder (pale, milk-
   fed veal)

1/2 pound pork sausage meat

1/2 cup instant brown rice (right out of the box)

1. Preheat the oven to 375°F. Coat a jelly-roll pan with nonstick cooking spray and set aside.
2. Using 8 to 10 staccato pulses, coarsely chop the pepper–onion mix with the chutney, curry powder, herb mix, salt, and pepper in a food processor fitted with the metal chopping blade. Tip into a large bowl.
3. Add the ground turkey, sausage, and rice, then using your hands, mix thoroughly. Scoop into the pan and shape into an oval loaf about 9 inches long, 5 inches wide, and 1½ inches high.

4. Bake in the lower third of the oven until an instant-read meat thermometer inserted in the middle of the loaf registers 170°F (160°F for veal), 45 to 50 minutes. Let the loaf rest 10 minutes.

5. Transfer the loaf to a heated serving platter, slice, and serve. Accompany, if you like, with additional chutney.

LITTLE THAI TURKEY LOAVES

MAKES 6 SERVINGS

Because I'm so fond of Thai food, I decided to build its dominant flavors—coconut, lemongrass, and cilantro—into a turkey loaf. Or rather into six individual loaves that bake in a muffin tin in just half an hour. By chopping the scallions, cilantro, lemongrass, and garlic together in a food processor I can do four jobs at one time—on fast-forward. Minus a processor (or electric blender), you'll have to hand-chop but this shouldn't take more than ten minutes. This recipe needs no salt or pepper.

6 medium scallions, trimmed and chunked (include some green tops)

1/3 cup packed fresh cilantro leaves

One 5-inch stalk lemongrass, cleaned and thickly sliced, or the zest of 1/2 medium lemon, removed in strips with a vegetable peeler

2 medium garlic cloves

1 pound ground turkey (preferably a 50-50 mix of light and dark meat)

1/2 cup instant brown rice (right out of the box)

One 14-ounce can unsweetened low-fat coconut milk

3/4 cup Thai peanut sauce

2 teaspoons Asian toasted sesame oil

1 tablespoon raw (turbinado) sugar

6 fresh cilantro sprigs (optional)

1. Preheat the oven to 400°F. Coat 6 muffin-pan cups with nonstick cooking spray and set aside.

2. Pulse the scallions, cilantro, lemongrass, and garlic 8 to 10 times in a food processor fitted with the metal chopping blade (or in an electric blender) until finely chopped.

3. Tip into a large bowl, add the turkey, rice, ½ cup each of the coconut milk and peanut sauce, and the sesame oil and mix thoroughly with your hands.

4. Pack the turkey mixture into the muffin-pan cups and bake until an instant-read meat thermometer inserted into the center of a loaf registers 170°F, 30 to 35 minutes.

5. Meanwhile, make a sauce by whisking the remaining coconut milk with the remaining peanut sauce and the sugar.

6. To serve, unmold the loaves onto a heated platter and sprig with cilantro, if desired. Pass the sauce—either at room temperature or slightly warmed.

TURKEY MOLE LOAF

MAKES 4 TO 6 SERVINGS

Tortilla chips, chili-seasoned canned diced tomatoes with green chilies, and ground sweet chocolate with cocoa (one of the newer supermarket staples) give this turkey loaf believable Mexican flavor—and no, the chocolate isn't too sweet. Its function is to mellow the tartness of the tomatoes and tame the fire of the chilies. This meatloaf goes together fast and is ready to serve in less than an hour. Accompany with a cool salad of tossed greens. Or perhaps vinaigrette-dressed avocado crescents and grapefruit sections.

> 1 pound ground turkey
> 2 cups coarsely crushed tortilla chips
> One 10-ounce can diced tomatoes and green chilies with chili seasonings
> $1/2$ cup water
> 4 medium scallions, trimmed and coarsely chopped (include some green tops)
> $1/2$ cup coarsely chopped fresh cilantro
> 2 tablespoons sweet ground chocolate with cocoa (see headnote)
> 1 tablespoon Basic Herb Mix (page 15)
> 1 teaspoon chili powder
> $1/2$ teaspoon salt

1. Preheat the oven to 375°F. Coat a jelly-roll pan with nonstick cooking spray and set aside.

2. Using your hands, thoroughly mix all ingredients together. Scoop into the pan and shape into an oval loaf about 9 inches long, 5 inches wide, and 1½ inches high.

3. Bake in the lower third of the oven until an instant-read meat thermometer inserted in the middle of the loaf registers 170°F, about 45 minutes. Let the loaf rest 10 minutes.

4. Transfer the loaf to a heated serving platter, slice, and serve.

PRESSED CHICKEN

MAKES 12 TO 14 SERVINGS

Some Southerners call this cool mold "Mayonnaise Chicken," but "Pressed Chicken" is more appropriate because I've stripped the recipe of its mayonnaise (except for half a cup of sandwich spread). I've lightened things in other ways, too. My dog-earred card file recipe calls for a pint of mayonnaise and another of heavy cream. I've upped the chicken broth and used 1 cup of half-and-half. To trim prep time, I let my food processor do the chopping. I also add solidly frozen peas to the mix and that saves another step—no need to cook them because they're tiny and tender. And there's a bonus: the frozen peas speed the gelling of the mold. My major short-cut, however, is substituting fully cooked chicken breast strips (the kind all supermarkets sell) for a tough old bird that must be stewed. Because the unflavored strips were sold out, I settled for the Italian-flavored and they worked just fine. Don't be daunted by the length of this recipe. It goes together fast, then demands nothing more than undisturbed fridge time.

NOTE: *The first time I made this recipe I forgot an important lesson I'd learned in food chemistry: walnuts contain tannin, which will react with metal and discolor food. When I unmolded my Pressed Chicken, it was mauve—not very appetizing. Luckily the color could be scraped off. The next time I used a glass ring mold and the Pressed Chicken was the color of country cream.*

TIP: *You can, if you like, substitute cooked turkey or veal for chicken.*

3 cups fat-free chicken broth

1 cup half-and-half

2 envelopes plain (unflavored) gelatin

1 cup walnuts

2 large celery ribs, trimmed and cut into 1-inch chunks

4 medium scallions, trimmed and cut into 1-inch chunks
    (include some green tops)

Two 10-ounce packages plain or Italian-flavored roasted
    chicken breast strips

One 8-ounce package light cream cheese (Neufchâtel),
    at room temperature

1/4 teaspoon freshly ground black pepper

1/2 cup sandwich spread (mayonnaise and pickle relish)

One 10-ounce package solidly frozen tiny green peas

2 tablespoons well-drained small capers

Salt, as needed

1. Lightly coat a 3-quart decorative glass or ceramic mold or ring mold with nonstick cooking spray and set aside.

2. Combine the chicken broth and half-and-half in a large saucepan, sprinkle the gelatin evenly on top, and let stand a few minutes. Stir well and set over lowest heat—by the time you've prepped the other ingredients, the gelatin will be dissolved and all you have to do in the interim is give it an occasional stir.

3. Meanwhile, pulse the walnuts in a food processor fitted with the metal chopping blade until moderately finely chopped; tip the nuts into a large mixing bowl. Pulse the celery and scallions until finely chopped (no need to wash the bowl or blade), and add to the bowl. Pulse the chicken strips in two batches until fairly finely chopped and add to the bowl.

4. Pour half of the hot gelatin mixture into the processor work bowl, add the cream cheese by pinching off small chunks, and the pepper, and churn until smooth— 8 to 10 seconds should do it. Pulse in the sandwich spread and add to the bowl along with the remaining gelatin mixture, the peas, and capers. Stir well, taste for salt, and adjust as needed.

5. Pour the chicken mixture into the mold, set uncovered in the refrigerator, and chill several hours or overnight until firm. I do not cover the mold because the gelatin mixture is hot and droplets of water may condense on the cover, then fall back into and soften the gelatin.

6. To unmold the Pressed Chicken, dip quickly in hot water, then invert on a colorful round platter. Garnish, if you like, with any colorful lettuces—radicchio, watercress, arugula. Cut into wedges and serve.

VARIATION

Pressed Turkey Prepare as directed, substituting 4 cups cooked turkey breast or veal for the chicken, adding 1 teaspoon Basic Herb Mix (page 15), and adjusting the salt and pepper as needed.

PARTY LOAF OF CIRCASSIAN CHICKEN

MAKES 12 SERVINGS

I tasted this unusual dish on my first trip to Turkey years ago and couldn't wait to try it back home. This was pre–food processor, so I pulverized the walnuts in a mortar and pestle as Turkish cooks had been doing forever. Needless to say, I didn't try the recipe again until I had a food processor—it reduced the prep time to seconds. I've short-cut the recipe further still by using the carved, roasted chicken breast strips now sold at every supermarket. True Circassian chicken is made by layering slices of poached chicken with walnut sauce, frosting the lot with more sauce, then squiggling on paprika oil à la Jackson Pollock. I've turned the recipe into a cool gelatin loaf that's perfect for a big summer luncheon accompanied by a tartly dressed salad of arugula, radicchio, and Belgian endive.

TIP: *I often slip roasted chicken breast strips into the freezer as soon as I buy them. They're easier to dice neatly; moreover, frozen chicken makes the mixture gel faster.*

4 teaspoons plain (unflavored) gelatin

2 1/4 cups chicken broth

1 pound shelled walnuts

4 slices firm-textured white bread, trimmed of crusts and soaked about 5 minutes in 1/3 cup half-and-half

1 small yellow onion, peeled and chunked

1 teaspoon Basic Herb Mix (page 15)

1/2 teaspoon celery salt

1/2 teaspoon salt

1/4 teaspoon freshly ground black pepper

Two 10-ounce packages carved, roasted chicken breast strips, coarsely diced

1/4 cup fruity olive oil blended with 2 teaspoons sweet paprika (paprika oil)

1. Lightly coat a 9 × 9 × 2-inch glass or ceramic baking dish with nonstick cooking spray and set aside. Do not use metal because your Circassian Chicken will turn purple.
2. Combine the gelatin and ¼ cup of the chicken broth in a small ramekin, stand in a small saucepan containing about 1 inch of water, and set over moderately low heat until the gelatin dissolves completely; this will take 8 to 10 minutes.
3. Meanwhile, reduce the walnuts, bread and soaking cream, onion, herb mix, celery salt, salt, and pepper to paste by churning in a food processor fitted with the metal chopping blade 15 to 20 seconds. Scrape the work bowl and pulse out any lumps. With the motor running, slowly pour the remaining chicken broth down the feed tube to form a thick sauce.
4. Scrape the walnut mixture into a large bowl, blend in the dissolved gelatin, then fold in the diced chicken. Scoop into the baking dish, spreading to the corners and smoothing the surface. Cover loosely with wax paper and refrigerate for several hours or until firm.
5. To serve, make a cut down the middle of the gelatin mixture from top to bottom, then make 5 crosswise cuts, dividing into 12 slices of equal size. TIP: *When cutting a gelatin mold, it helps if you dip your knife into hot water between cuts.*
6. Lay the slices of Circassian Chicken flat on bright luncheon plates, then using a small squirt bottle, zig-zag a little of the paprika oil on each slice (you can also drizzle the paprika oil from a teaspoon). Add some tartly dressed greens and serve.

FRESH SALMON LOAF WITH CUCUMBER-DILL SAUCE

MAKES 4 SERVINGS

Like most of us, I grew up on salmon loaves made of canned salmon. But with both fresh and smoked salmon now widely available, I decided to team the two in a loaf along with fresh dill—a supermarket staple right around the calendar.

SALMON LOAF

1 pound skinless fresh salmon fillets, coarsely chopped

1/4 pound sliced smoked salmon, coarsely chopped

1/2 cup coarsely crumbled soda crackers (12 two-inch-square crackers)

1/3 cup half-and-half

1 small yellow onion, finely chopped

1/2 medium green bell pepper, cored, seeded, and finely chopped

2 tablespoons snipped fresh dill or 1 teaspoon dried dill weed

1/4 teaspoon freshly ground black pepper

CUCUMBER-DILL SAUCE

One 6-ounce container plain low-fat yogurt

1 small cucumber, peeled, seeded, and finely diced

1 tablespoon snipped fresh dill or 1/2 teaspoon dried dill weed

1. SALMON LOAF: Preheat the oven to 350°F. Coat an 8½ × 4½ × 2¾-inch loaf pan with nonstick cooking spray and set aside.

2. Using your hands, thoroughly mix all ingredients in a large bowl, then pack into the pan.
3. Bake in the lower third of the oven until an instant-read meat thermometer inserted in the middle of the loaf registers 160°F, about 30 minutes. Cool the loaf in the upright pan on a wire rack for 10 minutes.
4. SAUCE: While the loaf is cooling, quickly whisk together the yogurt, cucumber, and dill, then scoop into a sauceboat.
5. Turn the salmon loaf out on a heated platter, cut into slices about 1 inch thick, and serve. Pass the sauce separately.

OLD-FASHIONED SALMON LOAF

MAKES 4 SERVINGS

Much more like the salmon loaf that I grew up on—only better because it's moister and spicier. Because of the saltiness of the salmon and sandwich spread, this recipe needs no additional salt. Serve with the Cucumber-Dill Sauce that accompanies the Fresh Salmon Loaf (page 233).

Two 7.5-ounce cans pink salmon, drained and liquid
    reserved
Salmon liquid plus enough cold water to total $^1/3$ cup
$^1/2$ cup $^1/2$-inch cubes firm-textured white bread
$^1/2$ cup sandwich spread (mayonnaise and pickle relish)
$^1/3$ cup half-and-half
1 small yellow onion, finely chopped
1 large egg
2 tablespoons snipped fresh dill or $^1/2$ teaspoon dried dill
    weed
$^1/4$ teaspoon freshly ground black pepper

1. Preheat the oven to 350°F. Coat a $7 \times 3^1/2 \times 2^1/2$-inch loaf pan with nonstick cooking spray and set aside.

2. Place the salmon in a large bowl and flake, removing dark bits of skin. Add all remaining ingredients, and using your hands, mix thoroughly. Pack the mixture into the pan. Or if you prefer, shape into a $7 \times 3^1/2 \times 2^1/2$-inch loaf on a baking sheet that has been spritzed with nonstick cooking spray.

3. Bake in the lower third of the oven until an instant-read meat thermometer inserted into the middle of the loaf registers 165°F, about 30 minutes.

4. Cool the loaf on a wire rack in the upright pan for 10 minutes, then slice right in the pan and serve with Cucumber-Dill Sauce.

PIMIENTO-SALMON LOAF

MAKES 4 SERVINGS

I particularly like the delicate flavor of this salmon loaf. I also like its flecks of red (pimiento) and green (parsley). The criss-cross of bacon isn't just cosmetic: the drippings trickling off the bacon baste the salmon loaf as it bakes and keep it moist.

Two 7.5-ounce cans pink salmon, drained and liquid
    reserved

2 cups soft white bread crumbs (page 19) or fresh cornbread
    crumbs

Salmon liquid plus enough milk or fat-free evaporated milk
    to total $1/2$ cup

2 large eggs

One 4-ounce jar diced pimientos, drained

4 medium scallions, trimmed and coarsely chopped
    (include some green tops)

$1/4$ cup coarsely chopped flat-leaf parsley

2 tablespoons well-drained small capers

Juice of $1/2$ medium lemon

1 teaspoon finely grated lemon zest

$1/4$ teaspoon freshly ground black pepper

2 slices uncooked bacon

1. Preheat the oven to 350°F. Lightly coat a small baking sheet with nonstick cooking spray and set aside.
2. Pick over the salmon, removing any dark skin, then flake and mix in a large bowl with all remaining ingredients except the bacon. Shape into a round loaf about 6 inches across on the baking sheet and criss-cross the slices of bacon on top.

3. Bake on the middle oven shelf until lightly browned and an instant-read meat thermometer inserted in the middle of the loaf registers 165°F, about 40 minutes.

4. Remove the loaf from the oven and let rest 10 to 15 minutes before serving.

CATFISH, COLLARDS, AND CORNBREAD LOAF

MAKES 4 SERVINGS

My aim here is to combine three of the South's favorite foods in a single loaf. It's an easy one-dish meal. I add no salt because the bacon and Cajun seasoning are plenty salty.

4 small skinless catfish fillets (about 1^1/2 pounds)

1 teaspoon Cajun seasoning

2 slices hickory-smoked bacon, stacked and snipped crosswise at ^{1}/2-inch intervals

1 small yellow onion, coarsely chopped

One 10-ounce package frozen chopped collards, thawed and drained

1 recipe Short-Cut Cornbread batter (page 34)

1. Preheat the oven to 425°F. Lightly coat a 9 × 9 × 2-inch baking pan with nonstick cooking spray. Rub both sides of each catfish fillet with Cajun seasoning, then arrange the fish in a single layer in the pan; set aside.

2. Sauté the bacon until crisp in a medium-size heavy skillet over moderate heat, then transfer to paper toweling to drain. Add the onion to the pan drippings and cook, stirring occasionally, until lightly browned, about 3 minutes. Add the collards and cook, stirring now and then, just until steaming, about 5 minutes. Remove from the heat.

3. Prepare the Short-Cut Cornbread batter as directed, then stir 1 cup of it into the collards mixture along with the reserved bacon and spread over the catfish. Top all with the remaining cornbread batter, spreading it to the corners.

4. Bake on the middle oven shelf until golden-brown and an instant-read thermometer inserted in the middle of the loaf registers 165°F, about 30 minutes.

5. Remove from the oven, let stand 5 minutes, then cut into large squares and serve.

MOLDED TUNA SALAD WITH FRESH DILL AND LIME

MAKES 6 SERVINGS

Far and away the quickest way to flake tuna is to do so right in the can. Once the tuna is drained, make a row of cuts in the tuna, spacing them about half an inch apart and cutting to the bottom of the can. Give the pan a quarter turn, and make a second row of cuts at right angles to the first. Fork the tuna into a mixing bowl and it should be just the right texture for this gelatin loaf. You can use any tuna, but my own favorite is solid white tuna (albacore) packed in water. This gelatin mold should be refrigerated overnight so that it has plenty of time to set up.

Two 12-ounce cans water-packed solid white tuna, drained
and flaked (reserve all liquid)

Tuna liquid plus enough chicken, vegetable, or clam broth to
total 2 cups

1 envelope plain (unflavored) gelatin

6 medium scallions, trimmed and moderately finely chopped
(include some green tops)

1 medium celery rib, trimmed and finely diced

3 tablespoons coarsely chopped fresh dill or 1 teaspoon
dried dill weed

3 tablespoons well-drained small capers

2 teaspoons Basic Herb Mix (page 15)

$1/4$ teaspoon freshly ground black pepper

$1/2$ cup regular or "light" mayonnaise (measure firmly
packed)

2 tablespoons fresh lime juice

1. Lightly spritz a 6-cup ring mold with nonstick cooking spray and set aside. Empty the flaked tuna into a large mixing bowl and set aside.

2. Place the tuna liquid mixture in a large, heavy nonreactive saucepan and sprinkle in the gelatin. Stir well, then set over low heat and cook, stirring occasionally, until the gelatin dissolves completely, about 5 minutes.

3. Meanwhile, add the scallions, celery, dill, capers, herb mix, and pepper to the bowl with the tuna and toss well to mix.

4. As soon as the gelatin has dissolved, remove from the heat and whisk in the mayonnaise and lime juice. Quick-chill by setting the pan in an ice bath (or in the freezer) until the liquid is syrupy. Add to the tuna mixture and mix well.

5. Pour into the ring mold, cover with wax paper, and set in the refrigerator overnight.

6. When ready to serve, dip the mold quickly in hot water, invert on a colorful round platter; if you like, sprig with radicchio and/or watercress or arugula. You might also add a few strategically placed wedges of lime.

CURRIED TUNA MOUSSE

MAKES 6 SERVINGS

Cool and refreshing on a hot summer day. What's best about this unusual mousse is that almost any liquid can be used—milk, cream, chicken broth, even peach or mango nectar. My favorite is fat-free evaporated milk because it tastes rich yet adds very few calories.

1 envelope plain (unflavored) gelatin

2 teaspoons curry powder

1 teaspoon Basic Herb Mix (page 15)

1 cup fat-free evaporated milk

$^1/_3$ cup "light" mayonnaise

$^1/_4$ cup finely minced mango chutney

One 12-ounce can chunk white tuna, drained well and fairly
finely flaked

$^1/_2$ cup heavy cream, whipped to soft peaks

3 tablespoons well-drained small capers

1. Lightly coat a 4- or 5-cup ring or decorative mold with nonstick cooking spray; set aside.
2. Combine the gelatin, curry powder, herb mix, and milk in a large nonreactive saucepan and let stand 5 minutes. Set over moderate heat and stir until the gelatin dissolves, about 3 minutes. Off heat, whisk in the mayonnaise and chutney. Set the pan in an ice bath (or the freezer) and quick-chill until the mixture is the consistency of unbeaten egg white.
3. Beat the gelatin mixture until frothy, then fold in the tuna, whipped cream, and capers. Scoop into the ring mold, cover with wax paper, and refrigerate several hours or until set.
4. To unmold, quickly dip the mold in hot water and invert on a colorful round platter. Sprig, if you like, with watercress or curly endive, cut into wedges, and serve.

BAKED ITALIAN CLUB SANDWICH LOAF

MAKES 4 TO 6 SERVINGS

What you'll need for this loaf is a boule—a round Italian country bread measuring eight to nine inches across. Or failing that, any same-size round of good chewy country bread. Most high-end supermarkets now carry a variety of artisanal breads in their bakery departments.

> **One 8- to 9-inch boule (round Italian bread) about 4 inches**
> **high and weighing about 20 ounces**
> **1/4 cup fruity olive oil**
> **2 cups loosely packed arugula leaves**
> **8 thin slices provolone cheese (about 6 ounces)**
> **4 ounces thinly sliced prosciutto**
> **4 thin slices smoked turkey breast (about 4 ounces)**
> **1 medium sun-ripened tomato, cored and thinly sliced**
> **(I prefer low-acid yellow tomatoes)**

1. Preheat the oven to 425°F.
2. Halve the bread horizontally and brush each cut surface generously with the olive oil. Arrange the arugula on the bottom half of the loaf, top with half of the provolone, overlapping the slices, then all of the prosciutto, turkey, and tomato, each time overlapping the slices as needed. Top with the remaining provolone, set the top half of the loaf in place, and press down hard.
3. Wrap the loaf snugly in heavy-duty aluminum foil, set on an ungreased baking sheet, and bake in the lower third of the oven for 30 minutes. Remove from the oven, press down hard on the foil-wrapped loaf, and let stand 10 minutes.
4. To serve, unwrap and cut into wedges. I find this loaf perfect for a fast lunch or supper.

LITTLE LOBSTER LOAVES

MAKES 6 SERVINGS

Most good supermarkets sell fresh cooked lobster meat and that's what you should use here. It's packed in containers much like lump crab. I find these lobster loaves the perfect main course for a light summer lunch.

> 3 cups (about 1 1/2 pounds) diced, cooked lobster meat
>
> 2 tablespoons fresh lemon juice
>
> 1/2 cup mayonnaise (use "light," if you like)
>
> 1 medium celery rib, trimmed and finely diced
>
> 1 large scallion, trimmed and finely chopped (include some green top)
>
> 1 tablespoon finely chopped fresh tarragon or 1/2 teaspoon crumbled dried leaf tarragon
>
> 1 teaspoon salt
>
> 1/8 teaspoon ground hot red pepper (cayenne)
>
> 1 to 3 tablespoons milk, if needed to moisten the lobster mixture
>
> 6 soft French bread rolls or hamburger buns, halved horizontally and lightly buttered

1. Place the lobster meat and lemon juice in a large nonreactive bowl, toss well, and let stand 30 minutes. Add all remaining ingredients except the milk and rolls and toss well. If the mixture seems dry, moisten as needed with a little milk. At this point, you can cover the lobster mixture and refrigerate for several hours—it will be better if you do.

2. When ready to serve, pile the lobster mixture on the bottom halves of the rolls, dividing the total amount equally, cover with the top halves, and accompany, if you like, with juicily ripe wedges of tomato.

5 *TO BE PERFECTLY HONEST,* this was the hardest chapter for me to write, the one that offered the greatest challenge, because I love meat and always have. I do, however, respect my vegetarian friends and it is because of them that I have created a couple of dozen quick loaves that are entirely meatless.

However, most do contain dairy—milk, cheese, and eggs—because it's virtually impossible to make a loaf without them. A few, moreover, are set with gelatin, which is made from calves' feet. So these two or three recipes would be off-limits for strict vegetarians.

Beans, greens, and grains are the vegetarian's best friend. Nuts and tofu, too. And when combined in the right proportions, these not only provide proper nourishment but also plenty of flavor.

Meatless Loaves

Like so many carnivores, I'd always assumed that vegetarian food was bland and blah. Not so, I quickly discovered while developing these meatless recipes. In fact, many of these quick-mix loaves, terrines, and puddings have such depth of flavor I'm entirely happy skipping meat—now and then.

My favorites are Spinach–Roasted Red Pepper Terrine, Broccoli-Scallion Bread Pudding with Dill and Sour Cream Sauce, Gorgonzola-Pasta Ring, and Tofu–Cashew Muffin Loaves with Soy Mayonnaise. But you may find others.

MUSHROOM AND PECAN LOAF

MAKES 4 SERVINGS

There are meatless "meatloaves" galore but few as delicious as this one—even I, a devout carnivore, like it. This particular recipe isn't for vegans because it contains dairy.

> Two 6-ounce packages sliced portobello mushroom caps, coarsely chopped
>
> 4 cloves garlic, minced
>
> 2 tablespoons olive oil
>
> One 8-ounce package cream cheese, softened
>
> 1 large egg
>
> 3/4 cup water
>
> 1/4 cup dry port, sherry, or red wine
>
> 1 cup finely chopped pecans
>
> 1 cup instant bulgur (tabbouleh)
>
> 1/2 cup grated Parmesan (page 18)
>
> 1/2 cup chopped flat-leaf parsley or 2 tablespoons parsley flakes
>
> 2 teaspoons fresh lemon thyme or 1/2 teaspoon crumbled dried leaf thyme
>
> 1 teaspoon Basic Herb Mix (page 15)
>
> 1/2 teaspoon salt
>
> 1/2 teaspoon freshly ground black pepper

1. Preheat the oven to 400°F. Spray an 8½ × 4½ × 2¾-inch ovenproof glass, ceramic, or other nonreactive loaf pan with nonstick cooking spray and set aside.

2. Cook the mushrooms and garlic in the oil in a large skillet over moderate heat (or microwave in a wax paper–covered ceramic casserole on HIGH) until the mushrooms are just tender, about 5 minutes, either way.

3. Meanwhile, beat the cream cheese and egg in a large bowl until combined. Gradually beat in the water and port. Add the mushroom mixture, pecans, bulgur, Parmesan, parsley, thyme, herb mix, salt, and pepper and mix well.

4. Pack the mixture into the pan and bake in the lower third of the oven until an instant-read meat thermometer inserted in the middle registers 165°F, 40 to 45 minutes. Let the loaf rest in the upright pan for 15 minutes.

5. Loosen the loaf around the edge with a thin-blade metal spatula and turn out on a heated platter. Using a very sharp knife, cut into slices about ¾ inch thick, and serve.

BROCCOLI-SCALLION BREAD PUDDING
WITH DILL AND SOUR CREAM SAUCE

MAKES 6 SERVINGS

I recently enjoyed a savory bread pudding at one of my favorite Chapel Hill restaurants—Carolina Crossroads in the Carolina Inn. Chef Brian Stapleton had just worked up a new spring menu and his vegetable bread pudding piqued my interest. It was so delicious I decided to develop a short-cut version that could be sliced and served as a light entrée. To save time (but only after the ingredient list revealed no scary additives), I used a frozen quiche mix and thawed it overnight in the refrigerator.

PUDDING

One 26-ounce container frozen broccoli-Cheddar pour quiche, thawed

8 large scallions, coarsely chopped

1/2 cup half-and-half

1/3 cup grated Parmesan (page 18)

1/4 cup coarsely chopped fresh dill or 1 teaspoon dried dill weed

1/4 teaspoon freshly grated nutmeg

7 cups loosely packed 1/2-inch cubes firm white bread (7 to 8 slices)

SAUCE

1/4 cup half-and-half

3/4 cup sour cream (use "light," if you like)

1 tablespoon freshly snipped dill or 1/2 teaspoon dried dill weed

1/2 teaspoon salt

1/4 teaspoon freshly ground black pepper

1. PUDDING: Preheat the oven to 350°F. Coat a 3-quart soufflé dish with nonstick cooking spray and set aside.

2. Combine the thawed quiche mix, scallions, half-and-half, Parmesan, dill, and nutmeg in a large bowl. Fold in the bread cubes.

3. Scoop all into the soufflé dish and bake in the lower third of the oven until an instant-read meat thermometer inserted in the middle of the pudding registers 165°F, about 1 hour. Let the pudding stand in the upright soufflé dish on a wire rack 10 minutes.

4. SAUCE: While the pudding is standing, gradually blend the half-and-half into the sour cream, add the dill, salt, and pepper, and continue stirring until smooth.

5. Carefully loosen the bread pudding around the edge with a thin-blade metal spatula and unmold on a heated round platter. Cut into wedges, spoon a little of the sauce over each portion, and serve.

CHEESE PUDDING MADE WITH WHOLE-WHEAT BREAD

MAKES 6 SERVINGS

When I was little, I loved the cheese strata that my mother made. It was pure comfort food. This slightly gutsier version bakes as a loaf that can be sliced. The two variations are strictly my own—my mother did not like and would not eat spicy food. Serve this loaf—or either of its variations—as the centerpiece of a light lunch or supper.

3 large eggs

1 cup milk

2 tablespoons melted butter

1/4 teaspoon salt

1/4 teaspoon ground hot red pepper (cayenne)

1/4 teaspoon freshly grated nutmeg

9 slices firm-textured whole-wheat bread, cut into 1/2 inch squares (5 cups)

8 ounces coarsely shredded sharp Cheddar

1 small yellow onion, finely chopped

1 small garlic clove, finely chopped

1. Beat the eggs lightly in a large bowl with the milk, butter, salt, cayenne, and nutmeg. Stir in the bread, cheese, onion, and garlic. Cover and refrigerate at least 2 hours but not more than 4 hours.

2. When ready to proceed, preheat the oven to 350°F. Line an 8½ × 4½ × 2¾-inch loaf pan with aluminum foil, placing the shiny side against the pan and allowing a 1-inch overhang all around; generously coat the foil with nonstick cooking spray.

3. Transfer the bread mixture to the pan and bake in the lower third of the oven until the pudding is puffed and golden and the interior has reached 165°F on an instant-read thermometer, 50 to 55 minutes.

4. Loosen the pudding from the sides of the foil, then holding onto the foil, lift the pudding onto a heated platter and pull the foil from under the loaf. Slice about 1¼ inches thick and serve hot.

VARIATIONS

Jalapeño-Jack Bread Pudding Prepare the main recipe as directed, substituting firm-textured white bread for whole-wheat and coarsely shredded jalapeño Monterey Jack for Cheddar. Also add 1 teaspoon ground cumin and 1 to 2 drops hot green or red pepper sauce.

Pimiento Cheese Bread Pudding Prepare the main recipe as directed but substitute firm-textured white bread for whole-wheat. Also substitute 4 finely minced scallions for the yellow onion and add 1 very well-drained 4-ounce can diced pimientos, 1 tablespoon each ketchup and Dijon mustard, and 1 teaspoon prepared horseradish.

BLONDE LASAGNA

MAKES 10 TO 12 SERVINGS

There's no meat in this lasagna, yet it's hearty enough for an army of teenagers. Make it an hour or two ahead of time, if you like, and refrigerate until ready to bake, but if you do, increase the initial baking time by 10 to 15 minutes. Unlike classic meat-and-tomato lasagnas, this one goes together fast thanks to oven-ready lasagna noodles, bottled Alfredo, and pesto sauces. But like them, it also bakes slowly.

If you have a thirteen-by-nine-inch baking pan that's three inches deep, by all means use it. Most are two inches deep, so instead of covering the lasagna with foil before it goes into the oven, I slide a baking sheet on top—the foil tends to sink into the cheese topping, stick, and make a mess. I also bake the lasagna on a sheet of foil lest it boil over.

4 cups half-and-half or 2 cups each half-and-half and milk

1/2 cup instantized flour

One 16-ounce jar Alfredo sauce

1/2 teaspoon salt

1/4 teaspoon freshly ground black pepper

1 cup grated Parmesan (page 18)

3 cups reduced-fat ricotta (measure firmly packed)

One 10-ounce jar sun-dried tomato pesto sauce

3 cups coarsely shredded mozzarella

3 large eggs

12 no-cook lasagna noodles (from a 9-ounce package)

1. Preheat the oven to 375°F. Lightly coat a 13 × 9 × 2-inch baking pan (or better yet, a 13 × 9 × 3-inch baking pan) with nonstick cooking spray and set aside.

2. Blend 1 cup of the half-and-half with the flour in a medium saucepan, then whisk in the remaining half-and-half, the Alfredo sauce, salt, and pepper. Set over moderately high heat and bring quickly to the boil, stirring often. As soon as the sauce thickens—a minute or so after it boils—remove from the heat and whisk in ½ cup of the grated Parmesan. Set this cheese sauce aside.

3. Combine the ricotta, tomato pesto sauce, remaining ½ cup grated Parmesan, 1 cup of the shredded mozzarella, and the eggs in a large bowl, beating until blended.

4. Smooth 1½ cups of the reserved cheese sauce over the bottom of the pan, add 4 lasagna noodles, arranging them crosswise in the pan, overlapping slightly, and pressing into the sauce. Smooth on half of the ricotta mixture, spread with another 1½ cups cheese sauce, and sprinkle with 1 cup of the shredded mozzarella. Add 4 more noodles, arranging as before, smooth on the remaining ricotta, and spread with 1 more cup of the sauce. Lay the last 4 noodles on top, arranging the same way, spread with the remaining sauce, and scatter the rest of the mozzarella on top.

5. Slide a large piece of heavy-duty aluminum foil onto the middle oven rack (to catch drips), then center the pan of lasagne on the foil. Slide a baking sheet on top of the lasagne, letting it rest on the rims of the pan. Bake for 1 hour, remove the baking sheet, and then bake until the lasagna is tipped with brown, 15 to 20 minutes longer.

6. Remove from the oven and let stand 20 minutes. Cut into large squares and serve.

OVERNIGHT LASAGNA
WITH TOMATOES AND ARTICHOKE HEARTS

MAKES 6 SERVINGS

Any lasagna noodles will work in this recipe because there's enough moisture to soften them during their overnight stay in the refrigerator. Because of the acid in the pasta sauce, it's best to use an ovenproof glass, ceramic, or other nonreactive baking pan. Because of the saltiness of the cheeses and pasta sauce, this recipe doesn't need additional salt.

> One 15-ounce container reduced-fat ricotta
> One 8-ounce package coarsely shredded mozzarella
> 1/2 cup soft white bread crumbs (preferably Italian bread crumbs)
> 1/4 cup grated Parmesan (page 18)
> 1 teaspoon Basic Herb Mix (page 15)
> 9 lasagna noodles (about 8 ounces)
> One 26-ounce jar tomato-based pasta sauce (any brand you fancy)
> One 9-ounce package solidly frozen artichoke hearts

1. Generously coat a $9 \times 7 \times 2\frac{1}{2}$-inch (11-cup) baking dish with nonstick cooking spray and set aside.

2. Combine the ricotta, $\frac{1}{2}$ cup of the mozzarella, the bread crumbs, 2 tablespoons of the Parmesan, and the herb mix in a medium bowl.

3. Break the lasagna noodles to fit the baking dish, reserving the ends that were broken off. Spread $\frac{1}{2}$ cup of the pasta sauce in the bottom of the baking dish and lay 3 noodles in the sauce. Top with the frozen artichoke hearts, the reserved lasagna ends, and 1 cup of the sauce. Lay in 3 more noodles, spread with the ricotta mixture, then add the final 3 noodles and the remaining sauce.

4. Cover with wax paper, then aluminum foil, and refrigerate overnight or for at least 8 hours.

5. When ready to bake the lasagna, preheat the oven to 375°F. Uncover the lasagna, discarding the wax paper. Generously coat one side of the foil with nonstick cooking spray and cover the baking dish, placing sprayed side down. Bake the lasagna for 20 minutes.

6. Remove the foil, sprinkle the lasagna with the remaining mozzarella and Parmesan, and bake uncovered until puffed and lightly browned, 25 to 30 minute. Serve at once.

INDIVIDUAL RICE AND CHEESE LOAVES WITH MUSHROOM SAUCE

MAKES 4 SERVINGS

This is the recipe to make when you have leftover rice—either white or brown. Failing that, use Chinese take-out rice so you don't have to cook it yourself.

LOAVES

2 cups cooked rice

1 cup coarsely shredded sharp Cheddar

$3/4$ cup milk (use fat-free evaporated milk, if you like)

$2/3$ cup fine dry bread crumbs

2 large eggs, lightly beaten

$1/4$ cup coarsely chopped flat-leaf parsley or
1$1/2$ tablespoons parsley flakes

1 medium scallion, trimmed and finely chopped (include some green tops)

1 teaspoon Basic Herb Mix (page 15)

$1/4$ teaspoon salt

$1/4$ teaspoon cracked black pepper

SAUCE

One 10-ounce package sliced white mushrooms

1 small yellow onion, finely chopped

2 tablespoons butter

3 tablespoons flour blended until smooth with 1$1/2$ cups dry white wine, or vegetable or chicken broth

Salt and freshly ground black pepper to taste

1. LOAVES: Preheat the oven to 350°F. Lightly coat four $4 \times 2\frac{1}{2} \times 1\frac{1}{2}$-inch loaf pans with nonstick cooking spray and set aside.

2. Mix all ingredients well in a large bowl, divide among the four pans, and set the pans on a baking sheet.

3. Bake in the lower third of the oven until an instant-read meat thermometer inserted into the middle of a loaf registers 165°F, 20 to 25 minutes. Cool the loaves upright in their pans on a wire rack 10 minutes.

4. SAUCE: When the loaves are baking or cooling, sauté the mushrooms and onion in the butter in a medium skillet over moderate heat until tender—about 5 minutes. Blend in the flour–wine mixture and cook, stirring often, until thickened, smooth, and no raw floury taste remains, about 5 minutes. Taste and add salt and pepper, if needed.

5. To serve, loosen the loaves around the edges with a thin-blade metal spatula and turn out on a heated platter. Pass the mushroom sauce separately.

GORGONZOLA-PASTA RING

MAKES 6 TO 8 SERVINGS

This delicious pasta ring may take an hour to bake, but it goes together zip-quick. Plan it for a party so that the platter's scraped clean. Leftovers, sad to say, are gummy, but that's the nature of pasta.

1 cup elbow macaroni

One 12-ounce can fat-free evaporated milk

3 large eggs

1 cup soft white bread crumbs (page 19)

3/4 cup finely crumbled Gorgonzola

1/4 cup grated Parmesan (page 18)

1/4 cup drained, diced bottled pimientos

1/4 cup coarsely chopped flat-leaf parsley

1/2 teaspoon finely chopped fresh rosemary or 1/4 teaspoon
    crumbled dried leaf rosemary

1/2 teaspoon salt

1/4 teaspoon ground hot red pepper (cayenne)

1. Preheat the oven to 350°F. Generously coat a 6-cup ring mold with nonstick cooking spray and set aside.
2. Cook the macaroni by package directions and drain well. Meanwhile, whisk the milk and eggs in a large bowl until well blended. Mix in all remaining ingredients, then the macaroni.
3. Scoop the mixture into the ring mold, smoothing the surface. Set the ring mold in a shallow roasting pan and slide onto the middle oven shelf. Pour enough hot water into the pan to come halfway up the sides of the ring mold.

4. Bake the pasta mold until set like custard and a cake tester inserted into the middle comes out clean, about 1 hour.

5. Carefully loosen the pasta mold with a thin-blade spatula, invert at once on a heated round platter, and serve.

SPINACH–ROASTED RED PEPPER TERRINE

MAKES 6 SERVINGS

My taste-testers couldn't get enough of this showy red and green vegetable terrine and refused to believe that it was a "quick and easy"—until I gave each of them the recipe. This terrine is good warm but even better cold, which makes it party-perfect. Slice about half an inch thick and overlap the slices on a red, yellow, or green platter. The terrine will be easier to unmold if you line the pan with foil. Here's how: invert a 9 × 5 × 3-inch loaf pan on the counter. Place a sheet of heavy-duty aluminum foil shiny-side-down on top of the pan, center it, then smooth the foil down over the pan, mitering the corners for a snug fit. Carefully lift the foil liner off of the pan, turn the pan right-side-up, and insert the foil liner, smoothing as needed to fit. Don't worry if there are a few wrinkles—these won't matter.

One 12-ounce jar roasted red bell peppers, well drained
1 medium garlic clove
$1/2$ cup instant couscous
$1/2$ cup boiling water
$1/4$ cup grated Parmesan (page 18)
1 teaspoon Basic Herb Mix (page 15)
$1/4$ teaspoon freshly ground black pepper
Three 12-ounce packages frozen spinach soufflé, thawed
overnight in the refrigerator

1. Preheat the oven to 400°F. Line a 9 × 5 × 3-inch loaf pan with aluminum foil as directed in the headnote, then coat generously with nonstick cooking spray and set aside.

2. Churn the drained red peppers and the garlic in a food processor fitted with the chopping blade until very finely chopped, 8 to 10 seconds. Scrape the work bowl, add the couscous, boiling water, Parmesan, herb mix, and black pepper and pulse to combine.

3. Spread half the thawed spinach soufflé in an even layer over the bottom of the prepared pan. Top with the red pepper–couscous mixture, again spreading in an even layer. Finally, smooth on the remaining spinach soufflé.

4. Bake uncovered on the middle oven shelf until an instant-read meat thermometer inserted in the center of the terrine registers 165°F, 65 to 75 minutes.

5. Cool the terrine in the upright pan on a wire rack 15 minutes, then invert on a heated platter and carefully peel off the foil liner. Let stand 10 minutes more, slice about ½ inch thick, and serve. Or, if you prefer, cover loosely with plastic food wrap, chill until firm, and serve cold.

MATZO-SPINACH LOAF

MAKES 6 SERVINGS

You can use any flavor of matzo here, but if they're salted, reduce the amount of salt in the recipe slightly. The baking pan you use must be at least two inches deep because this loaf puffs almost as dramatically as a soufflé. I like to ladle a little sour cream or yogurt over each portion, but if you want something a little fancier, use scallion or vegetable cream cheese thinned with sour cream or even better, sour cream with a little julienned smoked salmon stirred in.

> 3 large eggs
>
> 2 cups milk
>
> 3/4 teaspoon salt
>
> 1/2 teaspoon freshly ground black pepper
>
> Two 10-ounce packages frozen chopped spinach, thawed and
>   drained well
>
> One 8-ounce package coarsely shredded Swiss cheese
>
> 1 small yellow onion, finely chopped
>
> 1 teaspoon Basic Herb Mix (page 15)
>
> Five 6^1/2 × 6^1/4-inch plain, unsalted matzos

1. Generously coat an 8 × 8 × 2-inch pan with nonstick cooking spray and set aside.
2. Break the eggs into a medium bowl and whisk until frothy. Whisk in the milk, salt, and pepper. Remove 1½ cups of this mixture and set aside. Fold the spinach, ¾ cup of the cheese, the onion, and herb mix into the egg mixture remaining in the bowl.
3. Place 1 matzo in the pan and top with one quarter of the spinach mixture. Repeat three times, then top with the remaining matzo. Pour the reserved egg mixture evenly over all. Cover loosely with wax paper and let stand 15 minutes to allow the matzo to soften slightly. Meanwhile, preheat the oven to 375°F.

4. Remove the wax paper from the pan, then to break up the matzo slightly, push the end of a wide spatula or pancake turner down through the mixture, all the way to the bottom, in 8 to 10 spots. Also press and flatten the mixture with the spatula until it fills the pan and the liquid rises to the top.

5. Bake uncovered on the middle oven shelf for 20 minutes. Sprinkle with the remaining cheese and bake until puffed, lightly browned, and an instant-read meat thermometer inserted in the middle of the loaf registers 165°F, 25 to 30 minutes longer. Cut and serve at once, accompanying, if you like, with sour cream.

SPINACH AND PARMESAN TIMBALES

MAKES 8 SERVINGS

The perfect entrée for a light lunch but good, too, as a side dish. If you should have a couple of hard-cooked eggs on hand, chop them fine and add to the mix just before you spoon it into the ramekins. These timbales are good hot or at room temperature. And I even like them cold.

3 tablespoons olive oil

4 medium scallions, trimmed and coarsely chopped (include some green tops)

Two 10-ounce packages frozen chopped spinach, thawed, drained, and pressed dry

$1/4$ teaspoon freshly grated nutmeg

$1/4$ teaspoon ground hot red pepper (cayenne)

One 12-ounce can fat-free evaporated milk plus enough fresh whole milk to total 2 cups

$1/4$ cup unsifted all-purpose flour

$1/2$ cup grated Parmesan (page 18)

2 large eggs, lightly beaten with $1^{1}/4$ teaspoons salt

1. Preheat the oven to 350°F. Lightly coat eight 6-ounce ramekins or custard cups with nonstick cooking spray and set aside.

2. Heat the olive oil in a medium-size heavy skillet over moderately high heat 1 minute. Add the scallions and stir-fry 2 to 3 minutes until golden. Add the spinach, nutmeg, and cayenne and cook, stirring occasionally, for 3 minutes.

3. Meanwhile, blend ½ cup of the milk with the flour until smooth, then whisk in the remaining milk. Add to the spinach and cook and stir until thickened—about 3 minutes. Mix in the Parmesan and as soon as it melts, blend a little of the hot spinach mixture into the beaten eggs. Stir back into the skillet and immediately remove it from the heat.

4. Divide the spinach mixture equally among the ramekins, arrange them, not touching, in a shallow roasting pan, and slide onto the middle oven shelf. Pour enough hot water into the roasting pan to come halfway up the sides of the ramekins.

5. Bake the timbales until set like custard and a cake tester inserted into the middle of one comes out clean, about 30 minutes.

6. Remove the timbales from the oven and from the water bath and cool on a wire rack for 10 minutes.

7. Carefully loosen each timbale with a thin-blade spatula, then invert on heated dinner plates and serve. Sliced sun-ripened tomatoes are the perfect accompaniment.

GREEN BEAN AND WALNUT LOAF

MAKES 6 SERVINGS

Not being a vegetarian, I turn to Jeanne Lemlin's wonderful Vegetarian Classics *or* Simple
Vegetarian Pleasures *for inspiration whenever I want to go meatless. This loaf, liberally adapted
from one of her recipes, is an ideal main course for a light summer lunch or supper. Do please note,
however, that it not only contains dairy but also gelatin, which is made from calves' hooves.*

NOTE: *You can also make this loaf without gelatin but it will be too soft to slice. Still, it can
be molded into a loaf, then served as a cocktail spread. If omitting the gelatin, add the wine in Step
4 as soon as the beans are tender and proceed as the recipe directs.*

1/2 cup dry red wine or port

2 envelopes plain (unflavored) gelatin

1 cup walnuts

2 tablespoons olive oil

1 large red onion, coarsely chopped

One 16-ounce package solidly frozen French-style green
     beans

One 8-ounce package cream cheese, at room temperature

1/3 cup bottled black olive spread or tapenade (some
     tapenades contain anchovies, so read the label before
     buying)

1/4 cup lightly packed flat-leaf parsley sprigs

4 cherry tomatoes, halved

1/2 teaspoon salt, or as needed

1/4 teaspoon freshly ground black pepper

1. Line an $8\frac{1}{2} \times 4\frac{1}{2} \times 2\frac{1}{2}$-inch loaf pan with plastic wrap, then lightly coat the wrap with nonstick cooking spray. Or use an ovenproof glass, ceramic, or other nonreactive pan spritzed with cooking spray.

2. Combine the wine and gelatin in a small bowl and set aside.

3. Sauté the walnuts in 1 tablespoon of the olive oil in a medium-size skillet over moderate heat until lightly browned, about 4 minutes. With a slotted spoon, transfer the nuts to a food processor fitted with the metal chopping blade.

4. Add the remaining oil to the skillet, then the onion, and stir-fry until it begins to brown, 3 to 5 minutes. Mix in the beans, turn the heat down low, cover, and cook, stirring occasionally, until the beans are tender—about 5 minutes. Uncover and cook until all liquid evaporates, 4 to 5 minutes longer. Scoop in the wine mixture (it will be quite solid) and heat just until the gelatin dissolves, about 1 minute.

5. Transfer the bean mixture to the processor, add the cream cheese, black olive spread, parsley, cherry tomatoes, salt, and pepper. Process until very finely chopped.

6. Pack the mixture into the loaf pan; cover, and chill 6 to 8 hours or overnight.

7. Unmold on a serving platter; peel off the plastic wrap, slice 1 to $1\frac{1}{4}$ inches thick and serve.

VARIATION

Mock Chopped Liver Prepare as directed, omitting the black olive spread and adding 2 quartered hard-cooked eggs plus 2 tablespoons mayonnaise before processing.

TEX-MEX TOFU LOAF WITH HEATED SALSA

MAKES 8 SERVINGS

I've never fancied tofu but do adore "hot and spicy." So I thought that a vegetarian loaf brimming with the flavors of the old Southwest would make me accept—if not embrace—tofu. It did.

NOTE: *To drain salsa truly dry, put it in a fine-mesh sieve, set over in a bowl, and press out the liquid using a wooden spoon, pancake turner, or the bowl of a ladle.*

One 14- or 15-ounce block extra-firm tofu

2 tablespoons vegetable oil

6 large scallions, trimmed and thinly sliced (include some green tops)

One 16-ounce jar tomato salsa, drained as dry as possible and liquid reserved (see headnote)

1^1/2 cups whole-wheat bread crumbs (page 19)

^{1}/4 cup dry-roasted sunflower seed kernels

2 teaspoons chili powder

2 teaspoons ground cumin

Salt, as needed

2 large eggs

4 teaspoons all-purpose flour

1. Preheat the oven to 350°F. Generously coat a 9-inch round layer cake pan or pie pan with nonstick cooking spray and set aside.

2. Place the tofu in a large fine-mesh sieve and set over a large bowl. Cover with wax paper, weight with a heavy skillet or pie pan topped with heavy cans. Let stand 15 to 20 minutes.

3. Heat the oil in a large heavy skillet over moderately high heat 1 minute, add the scallions and stir-fry until they begin to wilt, 1 to 2 minutes. Remove the weights and wax paper from the tofu, and quickly press out any residual liquid. Finely crumble the tofu into the skillet with the scallions (the pieces should be about the size of lentils) and stir-fry until firm, 6 to 8 minutes.

4. Transfer the skillet mixture to a large bowl, then mix in the drained salsa, bread crumbs, sunflower seeds, chili powder, and cumin. Taste for salt and add, if needed. Mix in the eggs. Scoop the mixture into the cake pan and shape into a 9-inch round, mounding it slightly in the center.

5. Bake in the lower third of the oven until firm, lightly browned, and an instant-read meat thermometer stuck into the middle of the loaf registers 165°F, 45 to 50 minutes. Let the loaf rest for 5 minutes.

6. Meanwhile, add enough cold water to the reserved salsa liquid to total 1 cup, pour into a small saucepan, and whisk in the flour. Set over moderate heat and cook, stirring constantly, until thickened and no raw floury taste remains, about 5 minutes.

7. To serve, cut the tofu loaf into six wedges and top each portion with a little of the heated salsa.

TOFU-CASHEW MUFFIN LOAVES WITH SOY MAYONNAISE

MAKES 8 MUFFIN-SIZE LOAVES

When it comes to tofu, my guru is Deborah Madison, one of the cleverest cooks I know. This recipe was inspired by one in a dandy little book of hers called This Can't Be Tofu!

You can save yourself lots of time if you processor-chop the scallions and garlic together (five quick pulses should do it). Tip them out of the machine, then coarsely processor-chop the mushrooms using six pulses but scraping the work bowl after the first three. Empty out the mushrooms, add the cashews, and pulse ten to fifteen times until finely ground. Once the cashews are out of the machine, add the cilantro and coarsely chop with several staccato pulses. There's no need to wash, rinse, or wipe the work bowl between any of these stages.

LOAVES

One 14- or 15-ounce block extra-firm tofu

2 tablespoons peanut or vegetable oil

6 large scallions, trimmed and coarsely chopped (include
some green tops)

2 large garlic cloves, coarsely chopped

One 10-ounce package sliced mushrooms, coarsely chopped

1 1/2 cups soft white bread crumbs (page 19)

1 cup finely ground salted, roasted cashew nuts

1/3 cup coarsely chopped fresh cilantro

3 tablespoons Thai peanut sauce

3 tablespoons soy sauce

1 tablespoon Asian toasted sesame oil

1 large egg

> **1 cup light mayonnaise**
>
> **1 large scallion, trimmed and minced (include some green**
>   **tops)**
>
> **2 tablespoons soy sauce**
>
> **2 tablespoons moderately finely minced fresh cilantro**

1. Preheat the oven to 350°F. Generously coat 8 muffin-pan cups (in a 12-cup muffin pan) with nonstick cooking spray and set aside.

2. Place the tofu in a large fine-mesh sieve set over a large bowl. Cover with wax paper, weight with a heavy skillet or pie pan topped with heavy cans; let stand 15 to 20 minutes.

3. Heat 1 tablespoon of the peanut oil in a large heavy skillet over moderately high heat 1 minute, add the scallions and garlic, and stir-fry until they begin to wilt, 1 to 2 minutes. Add the mushrooms and cook, stirring occasionally, until their juices evaporate, 6 to 8 minutes. Transfer all to a large bowl.

4. Add the remaining peanut oil to the skillet and heat 1 minute. Remove the weights and wax paper from the tofu, and quickly press out any residual liquid. Finely crumble the tofu into the skillet (the pieces should be lentil-size) and stir-fry 6 to 8 minutes. Add to the bowl along with all remaining loaf ingredients and mix well. Scoop a scant ½ cup of the mixture into each of the 8 muffin-pan cups, packing lightly.

5. Bake in the lower third of the oven until lightly browned and an instant-read meat thermometer stuck into the middle of a loaf registers 165°F, 35 to 40 minutes. Cool the loaves in the pan 10 minutes. Meanwhile, combine all Soy Mayonnaise ingredients.

6. To serve, ease the muffin loaves onto heated plates, allowing one or two per person, and spoon a little of the mayonnaise onto each plate.

QUESADILLA LOAVES

One nine-ounce package will give you twelve six-inch tortillas—exactly what you need for this recipe. I prefer the white corn tortillas, which soften as they bake and taste just like freshly made Mexican tortillas. It's important to grease the foil well because if you don't, the tortillas will stick fast. Use vegetable shortening or unflavored nonstick cooking spray.

One 9-ounce package 6-inch tortillas
2 cups coarsely shredded jalapeño Jack cheese
3/4 cup fresh or frozen corn kernels, thawed
One 16-ounce jar salsa (as hot and spicy as you like)
**1 medium firm-ripe Hass avocado, peeled, pitted, and thinly
    sliced**
Sour cream (optional; use reduced-fat, if you like)

1. Preheat the oven to 450°F. Very generously grease two 12 × 15-inch sheets of aluminum foil.
2. On one sheet of foil, layer 1 tortilla, ⅓ cup cheese, 2 tablespoons corn, a second tortilla, 3 tablespoons salsa, and ¼ of the avocado. Repeat once and then top with another tortilla, another layer each of cheese and corn. Top with a final tortilla. Set the quesadilla loaf aside, unwrapped. Make a second quesadilla loaf exactly the same way, then spoon half of the remaining salsa over each loaf.
3. Tightly wrap each loaf in the foil, then place the loaves on a jelly-roll pan and bake in the lower third of the oven for 20 minutes.
4. Gently unwrap each loaf (beware of the steam!), quarter, and serve, if you like, with sour cream.

EGG SALAD SANDWICH LOAF

MAKES 6 SERVINGS

Here's the way I hard-cook eggs and it's never failed me: place the eggs in a large heavy saucepan, add just enough cold water to cover them, and set over moderate heat. As soon as the water actively boils, remove the pan from the heat, cover, and let stand 15 minutes. Drain the eggs and cover with ice water. Crack the butt (rounded end) of each egg, then roll the eggs on the counter to loosen the shells. (Eggs will peel more neatly if they are not absolutely fresh—I choose those nearing the expiration date on the carton.) As for chopping the eggs, you can quarter them and pulse quickly in a food processor. Or you can use an old-fashioned egg slicer, slicing the eggs one way, giving them a quarter turn, then slicing again. This sandwich loaf can be served straight away, but it will be even better if you chill it for several hours.

8 hard-cooked large eggs, cooled, peeled, and coarsely
 chopped (see headnote)
1/2 cup bottled ranch salad dressing
1/3 cup coarsely chopped pimiento-stuffed green or pitted
 oil-cured ripe olives
1 tablespoon Dijon mustard
1/2 teaspoon Basic Herb Mix (page 15)
Salt, as needed
One 8- to 9-inch boule (round Italian bread) about 4 inches
 high, weighing about 20 ounces
2 cups shredded romaine or other lettuce (4 to 5 leaves with
 ribs removed)

1. Mix the eggs, dressing, olives, mustard, and herb mix in a medium bowl. Taste for salt and add, if needed.

2. Slice the loaf crosswise into 4 rounds about 1 inch thick. Place the bottom round on a serving plate, spread with ⅓ of the egg salad, and add ⅓ of the lettuce. Top with the next bread round, pressing firmly. Repeat twice, then set the top of the loaf in place.

3. Cut the loaf into 6 wedges and serve, or better yet, wrap tightly in foil or plastic wrap and refrigerate several hours before serving.

BAKED SOURDOUGH LOAF OF ROASTED RED PEPPERS, MARINATED MUSHROOMS, AND ARTICHOKE HEARTS

MAKES 4 TO 6 SERVINGS

My supermarket now stocks an appetizing array of marinated mushrooms and artichoke hearts, and I use both in this quick vegetarian sandwich loaf. To save time, I use quartered artichoke hearts and to pump up flavor, marinated mixed mushrooms.

> **One 8- to 9-inch round sourdough loaf about 4 inches high, weighing about 20 ounces**
>
> **One 10-ounce jar marinated mixed mushrooms, drained and 2 tablespoons liquid reserved**
>
> **One 6.5-ounce jar marinated quartered artichoke hearts, drained and 2 tablespoons liquid reserved**
>
> **2 tablespoons fruity olive oil**
>
> **8 thin slices provolone (about 6 ounces)**
>
> **1 cup tissue-thin slices finocchio (fennel; include some green tops)**
>
> **1 cup well-drained roasted red peppers (from a 12-ounce jar)**

1. Preheat the oven to 425°F.
2. Slice the bread horizontally into three layers of equal thickness. Quickly combine the reserved mushroom and artichoke liquids with the olive oil, then brush each cut surface generously with the mixture. Arrange half the provolone on the bottom layer and top with half each of the finocchio, mushrooms, artichoke hearts, and red peppers. Set the middle layer on top, then add the remaining provolone, finocchio, mushrooms, artichoke hearts, and red peppers. Set the top bread layer in place, and press down hard.

3. Wrap the loaf snugly in heavy-duty aluminum foil, set on an ungreased baking sheet, and bake in the lower third of the oven for 30 minutes. Remove from the oven, press down hard on the foil-wrapped loaf, and let stand 10 minutes.

4. Unwrap the loaf, then insert long decorative toothpicks into the loaf to mark off six wedges of equal size (the frilly toothpick tops should be plainly visible). Divide the loaf into wedges by cutting between the toothpicks. When serving, leave the toothpicks in place but do warn everyone to remove them before taking a bite.

MOLDED CHEDDAR MOUSSE

MAKES 8 TO 10 SERVINGS

I don't find that packaged grated cheeses melt very smoothly, so I choose a well-aged sharp Cheddar for this recipe and shred it fine using the food processor. I like to serve this mousse as the main course of a light lunch or supper. For a pretty presentation, fill the center with a green salad.

**2 envelopes plus 1 teaspoon plain (unflavored) gelatin
softened in $1/2$ cup water
One 12-ounce can fat-free evaporated milk
3 cups finely shredded sharp Cheddar (about $3/4$ pound)
2 tablespoons finely grated yellow onion
1 tablespoon tomato ketchup
1 tablespoon Dijon mustard
$1/2$ teaspoon salt
$1/4$ teaspoon ground hot red pepper (cayenne)
One 4-ounce jar diced pimientos, drained very dry
$1^1/2$ cups heavy cream, softly whipped**

1. Lightly coat a 6-cup ring mold with nonstick cooking spray and set aside.
2. Heat and stir the softened gelatin and milk in a double boiler top directly over moderate heat until the gelatin dissolves completely, 2 to 3 minutes. Set over simmering water, add the cheese, onion, ketchup, mustard, salt, and cayenne and cook, stirring frequently, until the cheese melts and the mixture is smooth, 4 to 5 minutes. Off heat, mix in the pimientos, then fold in the whipped cream until no streaks of orange remain.

3. Scoop into the ring mold, cover loosely with wax paper, and refrigerate several hours, or better yet overnight, until firm.

4. To unmold, dip briefly in hot water, and invert on a colorful round platter. Cut into wedges and serve with a tartly dressed green salad and crusty chunks of bread.

BROCCOLI PERFECTION SALAD

MAKES 6 TO 8 SERVINGS

The 1905 classic has been updated to take advantage of the slaw mixes now available in the produce section of every supermarket. I've chosen broccoli slaw for two reasons: it's more colorful than cabbage slaw, and more nutritious, too. This gelatin salad will firm up faster if you pour the mixture into an ice-cold mold (give it an hour in the freezer). Adding ice water to the gelatin mixture as I've done here also helps, as does quick-chilling the filled mold in an ice bath before it goes into the refrigerator. Ten minutes is about right.

> **2 envelopes plain (unflavored) gelatin**
> **3/4 cup cold water**
> **3/4 cup boiling water**
> **1/2 cup raw (turbinado) sugar**
> **3/4 teaspoon salt**
> **1 cup ice water**
> **1/2 cup cider vinegar**
> **One 12-ounce package broccoli slaw (broccoli, carrots,**
> **red cabbage)**
> **One 4-ounce jar diced pimientos, well drained**

1. Soften the gelatin in the 3/4 cup of cold water. Add the boiling water, sugar, and salt and stir until the gelatin dissolves. Mix in the ice water and vinegar, then fold in the broccoli slaw and pimientos.
2. Rinse an 8-cup decorative mold with cold water, then shake out the droplets. Ladle the broccoli mixture into the mold.

3. Cover with wax paper (not plastic wrap, which may trap condensed moisture and thin the gelatin). Chill several hours until firm or better yet, overnight.
4. Just before serving, dip the mold quickly in hot water, place a round platter on top of the mold, invert, and give a quick shake to loosen the salad. Cut into wedges and serve.

WALES SALAD

A joke in my family was that Daddy would not marry Mother unless she agreed to serve him salad every day. Back then, "salad" usually meant something made with gelatin and often it was as sweet as dessert. This salad, my father's favorite, is more savory than sweet. I have no idea where the name originated—perhaps Mother called it "Wales Salad" because it always salved Daddy's "dour Welsh streak."

1 envelope plain (unflavored) gelatin

$1/3$ cup cold water

$1/3$ cup boiling water

$1/3$ cup fresh lemon juice

3-ounce light cream cheese (Neufchâtel), at room
temperature

2 tablespoons sugar

$1/4$ teaspoon salt

$3/4$ cup half-and-half

1 cup coarsely shredded sharp Cheddar

1 cup sliced almonds

1 cup olive salad (sliced pimiento-stuffed olives),
well drained

1. Soften the gelatin in the cold water. Add boiling water, stir until the gelatin dissolves, then mix in the lemon juice.
2. Cream the Neufchâtel cheese, sugar, and salt in a medium bowl until smooth. Gradually stir in the gelatin mixture and the half-and-half. Fold in the shredded Cheddar, almonds, and olive salad.

3. Rinse a 4- or 5-cup decorative nonreactive mold with cold water, then shake out the droplets. Ladle the gelatin mixture into the mold. Cover with wax paper and chill several hours until firm or chill overnight.
4. Just before serving, dip the mold quickly in hot water, place a round platter on top of the mold, invert, and give a quick shake to loosen the salad. Cut into wedges and serve.

INDEX